Breaking the Glass Box

Breaking the Glass Box

A Korean Woman's Experiences of Conscientization and Spiritual Formation

JungJa Joy Yu

Foreword by
Rosemary Radford Ruether

WIPF & STOCK · Eugene, Oregon

BREAKING THE GLASS BOX
A Korean Woman's Experiences of Conscientization
and Spiritual Formation

Copyright © 2013 JungJa Joy Yu. All rights reserved. Except for brief quotations in critical publications or reviews, no part of this book may be reproduced in any manner without prior written permission from the publisher. Write: Permissions, Wipf and Stock Publishers, 199 W. 8th Ave., Suite 3, Eugene, OR 97401.

Wipf and Stock
An Imprint of Wipf and Stock Publishers
199 W. 8th Ave., Suite 3
Eugene, OR 97401

www.wipfandstock.com

ISBN 13: 978-1-62564-548-7

Manufactured in the U.S.A.

Contents

Foreword by Dr. Rosemary Radford Ruether | vii
Acknowledgments | xi

Chapter 1
Introduction | 1

Chapter 2
The Invisible Glass Box:
Interpersonal Conflicts of Korean Women | 14

Chapter 3
The Visible Glass Box: Conscientization
and Korean Women's Awareness of Oppression | 37

Chapter 4
Breaking the Glass Box: Spiritual Formation and
Contemplative Practice through Conscientization
for Korean Women | 60

Chapter 5
A New Cultural Paradigm for Breaking the Glass Box:
JungJa Joy Yu's Sticky Rice Effect—A Korean Woman's
Jeong-Filled Spirituality | 87

Chapter 6
Conclusion | 100

Bibliography | 111

Foreword

THIS BOOK, BREAKING THE *Glass Box*, clearly and powerfully analyzes the historical and cultural pattern of women's oppression in Korean culture and society. This culture of oppression is deeply rooted in millennia of Korean society that has shaped the family, work, religion, and the media. The religious traditions of Buddhism and Confucianism that dominated Korean society for more than a thousand years (918–1910 C.E.) reinforced its patriarchal culture. Confucianism particularly mandated dualistic social hierarchies of rulers over subjects, husbands over wives, older siblings (especially brothers) over younger siblings (especially sisters) and men over women. Seven rules were laid out for a woman: to be obedient to her parents-in-law, to give birth to a son, not to be talkative, not to commit adultery, not to be jealous of her husband's concubine, not to carry a malignant disease, and not to commit theft. Quiet subjugation to her subordinate position in the household was woman's lot in marriage.

Christianity has come to dominate (South) Korean society in the twentieth century. Although potentially carrying a message of liberation and equality for all, it has in fact been incorporated into Korean patriarchal culture. It has been contemptuous of indigenous Korean culture, but it has accepted its patterns of male domination, which also came with it in another version from the West. Even though Korean women have accepted Christianity enthusiastically—70 percent of Korean Christians being women—the churches either reject or discourage women's ordination and demand that they be silent in church.

But these patterns of women's oppression have begun to change in Korean society. Modernization has brought equal education to women with men. Although still male-dominated, women are entering the work force and are becoming more prominent in professional jobs. The demands of the church and society that women be subordinate have increasingly come into conflict with women's status in education and employment. Yet the belief that men are more valuable than women is still deeply ingrained in how men and women are socialized. Few women dare to openly criticize this view.

JungJa Joy Yu speaks of this culture and social pattern of women subordination as the "invisible glass box." It is invisible because it is not openly acknowledged, and yet it is there, shaping women's reality in all parts of their lives in Korean society. It calls for her to sacrifice herself to her parents, to her husband and to her children. It is a glass box with no door, because there is no evident way out of it.

Through education and new experiences Korean women are becoming aware of this oppressive glass box. The glass box is changing from being invisible to being a visible glass box. Feminist theology particularly is a key tool for Korean Christian women to become aware of the glass box and to begin to question its ideological control over their lives. Third world feminist theology has added to the tools of Korean women's conscientization by putting the issues of women's oppression in the context of third world societies and their experience of colonialism and post-colonialism. Korean women are beginning to gain a language to critique the way they have been subjugated and to facilitate the process of waking up from this subjugation and freeing themselves from it.

JungJa Joy Yu sees two interlocked aspects of Korean culture as keys to women's subjugation and liberation. These are the deep patterns of *han* and *jeong*. *Han* is the culture of oppression and resentment of oppression. It is negative emotional and psychological energy that pervades Korean culture, boxing women and men into

Foreword

the system of patriarchy. *Jeong* means love, relationship, affection, and positive emotional and psychological energy. It can become liberating, but without being freed from *han*, it remains a tool of being tied to *han*, of sacrificing yourself to others.

As JungJa Joy Yu puts it, "*jeong* and *han* can be understood together through their historical background. Through many national crises Korea has endured its people have attained a spirit of caring or holding on, which can be described as a special bonding or companionship between people and things they shared in such difficult times together. It is because Koreans have experienced *han*-ridden challenges all of their lives, economically, politically, and socially throughout their history. Subsequently, Koreans have special affection toward people and physical things or stuff when they are symbols of strong relationships of commitment through thick and thin together in the form of the presence of *jeong*." (see page 44).

The interconnection of *han* and *jeong* continues to tie a Korean woman to patterns of subjugation and lack of self-esteem. JungJa Joy Yu feels herself to have been a product of this pattern of feelings. As the youngest child and daughter in her family, she was very much supported in her education by her parents. She was able to go to the best universities and was highly successful in her studies. Yet she was made to feel guilty and unsuccessful because she had not gotten married or had children. In seeking ordination, she was told by Korean male pastors that she was not acceptable as a leader in the church because she was a woman. These conflicting emotions of feeling inadequate and a failure have shaped her life.

Thus JungJa Joy Yu seeks to move to a third stage, from naming the glass box and making it visible to the liberating process of "breaking the glass box." Breaking the class box or dissolving it, so one can emerge from it, is the key process of women's emancipation. Korean women must learn to accept elements of conflict and anger as a legitimate part of freeing themselves from demands of subordination and marginalization. They must recognize themselves as agents of change of their own lives, not waiting for parents or church leaders to do this for them. They must also reimage their concept of God. They must overcome the idea of God as

Foreword

oppressive patriarchal punisher. Instead, they must see God as a healer and liberator who affirms the goodness of their humanity.

Jeong or loving relationship has to be freed from *han* and become a force for building community between peoples, especially between women, who are creating and liberating solidarity together. JungJa Joy Yu speaks of such communities of liberating solidarity as "sticky rice" communities. "Sticky rice" means rice that is shared and that brings people together in mutual affirmation. Our self-criticism needs to be transformed into self-confidence. We need to become kind to ourselves and find an inner mentor and champion in ourselves, supported by our experience of God as liberating friend.

This process of self-liberation and community building in relationships of solidarity is an ongoing process. It may never be completely finished. But it allows Korean women to grow in a way that is no longer blocked by gnawing feelings of inadequacy and guilt. It is a way of building a holistic Korean women's spirituality, both for themselves and in new communities of solidarity. These communities must become diverse and intercultural, linking liberated Korean women with other friends in solidarity across the world. This is the culmination of JungJa Joy Yu's vision of the process of liberation. By naming the glass box, making it visible and finally breaking it and transforming it into sticky rice communities of solidarity, she moves into an ongoing process of liberating community building for an alternative life and world.

Dr. Rosemary Radford Ruether
Claremont School of Theology and Claremont Graduate University

Acknowledgments

MOST OF ALL, I thank God for my life challenges, and for my academic and ministry experiences at Fuller Theological Seminary and Claremont School of Theology, which helped produce this book as my first voice to the world. I thank Dr. Rosemary Ruether, an author of forty-seven books and a professor of fifty years, for her encouragement and support to publish this book, for her recommendation, foreword, and her exemplary life as a feminist scholar. I thank Allison Becker—a Christian artist and minister who graduated from Fuller Theological Seminary and who is passionate about ministries of teaching, preaching, and worship—for contributing five pieces of wonderful illustrations for my book. I thank Dr. Theresa Yugar and Ann Hidalgo, feminist scholars, for their support and encouragement, which helped bring my ideas of breaking the glass box and sticky rice to this book.

I thank the professors of Claremont School of Theology. I thank Dr. Frank Rogers, my main supervisor for my MA thesis, for providing great teaching and wisdom on the oppressive culture in Korea. I thank Dr. Andrew Dreitcer, my academic advisor and supervisor for my MA thesis, for helping me engage contemplative practices as healing methods for Korean women. I thank Dr. Sam Lee, Dr. Helene Slessaver-Jamir, and Dr. Sheryl Kujawa-Holbrook, for helping me find the disciplines for my thesis. I thank the professors of Fuller Theological Seminary. I thank Dr. Veli-Matti Kärkkäinen and Dr. Caroline Gordon, for their consistent support during my academic journey. I thank the staff of Wipf and Stock

Acknowledgments

Publishers, K.C., Christian, Laura, William, Caitlin, Matt, Ian, and so on, for their hard work in publishing it.

I thank DSF friends, including Dr. Jon Berquist, Dr. Jo Ann Bynum, and Dr. Mark Parson, who encouraged my academic journey. I thank Rev. Julie-Roberts Fronk and Rev. Mike Fronk, and the choir and church members of my church in Pomona, including Lois and Rhodes Thomson, Beverly and Edward Burton, Elaine and Tom Reed, Jan and Ray Akin, Nancy and Laddie, Ginger, Ken, Carol, Christi, Jane, Linda, Julie and Bob, Jeffrey, Donna, Lucy, and so on, who have prayed for me and read my thesis as my first audience. I thank many ministers, including Rev. Susan and Rev. Don Dewey, Rev. Geun Hee and Guen Soon Yu, Rev. Jinsuk Chun and Rev. Myung-Sun Cheon, Rev. Young and Jun Kim, Rev. Christina Kang, Rev. Paul and Maria Im, and Rev. Shalom Kim, for supporting my journey to become a minister.

I thank many friends in the CST community, including Betty Frank, Patrick Reyes, Martha Barcenas, Lynn Oleary-Archer, Lea Appleton, Nancy Sample, Wally, Susan Holden, Vashti Arguijo, Joseph, Pam, Adam, Vernon, and Mary Pearce who have read my thesis and who have also had great conversations on the topic. I thank my Fuller Theological Seminary community and friends who supported my studies during and after my Mdiv degree, including Terry, Marlene, Sharon, Krissy, Kristi and Bob, Ingrid, Hanne, Sheridan, Paul, and so on, with their encouragement, prayers, and supports.

I thank my Korean friends, Youngju Lee, Yoon-Hee Hwang, Eun-Hee Lee, E. J. Hong, Kwang-Uk Lee, and Misun Chun, and Grace Kang, for their consistent encouragement and friendship. I thank so many friends whom I cannot name, because of the limit of paper, for supporting and encouraging me in so many ways in Korea, in America, and in many other countries.

I thank my family members: my father in heaven, In-Ok Yu, and my mother, Ann-ym Kim, and my siblings and their spouses, Chong-Ryeol and Yeon-Oh, Kyung-Ja and Ki-Soo, Young-Ryeol and Mi-Hwa, Bong-Ryeol and Young-Soon, and my nephews and nieces, Kyung-Soo, Hyo-Jeong, Jae-Jin, Sun-Joo, Meong-Joo, Jae-Sung, Ka-Hyun, Ka-Eun, Jae-Woong, and Se-In.

Chapter 1

Introduction

THIS BOOK EXAMINES THE interpersonal conflicts that contemporary Christian Korean women endure in Korean culture, churches, and society, and it uncovers how these interpersonal conflicts inhibit Korean women's full participation in church and society. In it, I propose a process of spiritual formation that can be used to help Korean women overcome the psychological oppression of the patriarchal attitudes, ideologies, and behaviors within Korean culture that inhibit their full liberation. Though in contemporary times, most educated Korean women do not associate the terms "oppression" and "liberation" with sexual or physical abuse and freedom from it, I suggest that more broadly what they experience is the gender discrimination of a *han*-based group culture. Among Koreans, *han* represents oppressive elements of Korean society that inadvertently affect the empowerment and disempowerment to Korean women. *Han* has been defined as a communal psychological construct that results from society's oppressive manipulation and control over women as a group.

The image of "breaking the glass box"[1] has resulted from the liberation process from my personal experiences of gender

---

1. I coin this term based on my personal experiences of oppression in Korean culture. For me, the metaphor of a glass box reflects the multiplicity of ways that I, as a Korean woman, have been oppressed by and liberated

1

oppression, through my multiple awareness practices of conflicts in Korean culture. Those practices include consciousness-raising, which has in turn helped me to discern the reasons for interpersonal conflicts in Korean socio-cultural contexts. The metaphor of breaking the glass box includes the transparent process from the dark-glass box before it is broken. In the process of making transparent the dark glass box, the stages of awareness are significant. By bringing such transparency to my situation, I realized I had been marginalized without knowing it; I had never understood myself to be a victim of sexism. When I finally became aware that I was living in an oppressive culture, I still could not break out of it because I had internalized the culture.

Yet, awareness did not immediately bring with it liberation; because it was a part of who I was, I did not know how to get out of it. So I stayed in the glass box. How could I leave the oppression behind without also losing my identity as a Korean woman? As a glass box with no door, the only way to get out of it was to break it, not in violent ways but with nonviolent spiritual practices and active faith that I refer to as *praxis*. Although nonviolent, such praxis-oriented liberative actions and attitudes caused interpersonal conflicts, specifically acute discomfort for those around me. In the clash between the controlling ethos of my culture and my desire to be free of it, my culture marginalized me and identified me as a troublemaker. Despite this, I was determined to stay the course. Only through the consistent and persistent practices of exploring who I truly was and what was important to me, I was able to find my true identity in Christ and speak with my own voice about Korea's culture of oppression. This liberation process has emerged as an important part of my own spiritual journey. This spiritual journey has required me to face and overcome many elements of oppression ingrained in Korean society.

Korean women's oppression stems from misogyny, "the hatred of women," that includes sexual discrimination, denigration

---

from patriarchal socio-religious-cultural standards for women within Korean culture and churches.

of women, violence against women, and sexual objectification.[2] In his *Dictionary of Sociology*, Allan G. Johnson agrees with the traditional definition of misogyny as "a cultural attitude of hatred for females because they are female,"[3] and argues that misogyny is a "core part of sexist prejudice" that is grounded in male-dominated societies. That misogyny manifests itself in many ways, "from jokes to pornography to violence to the self-contempt women may be taught to feel toward their own bodies."[4] As elsewhere, so in Korea, women and men are easily indoctrinated through the media with distorted representations of women, particularly by the media's objectification and commodification of female bodies. This leads many men to oppress women and others with less power, often through sexual harassment and violence.

The reach of the media extends beyond men, of course, to influence the entire culture, including the expectations of women themselves. In this respect, Korean women face the challenge of sexual discrimination through the media that objectifies women as sexual objects. In consideration of the huge influence of media in contemporary Korean society, K-pop stars, friends, media, and even their mothers tell them that pursuing beauty and perfection are the primary ways for them to be accepted in Korean society, if they want to avoid misogyny and traditional experiences of women in Korean patriarchal culture. For instance, because young women grow up believing the messages through media that they will "never find love or have a successful career if they are not beautiful," cosmetic surgery has become a popular high school graduation gift.[5] Relative to its population size, South Korea currently performs the largest number of plastic surgeries in the world. According to statistics reported in a 2010 survey by the International Society of Aesthetic Plastic Surgeons (ISAPS), "while the total number of aesthetic surgical procedures carried out was highest in the US, when the data was adjusted for population size,

2. Code, *Encyclopedia of Feminist Theories*, 346.
3. Johnson, "Misogyny."
4. Ibid.
5. Sherrd, "An Ugly Reflection."

it was revealed that for every 1000 Koreans, 16 had undergone plastic surgery of some description."[6]

A woman's expectations go far beyond her appearance. Every Korean woman struggles with losing her sense of being as an independent entity, because she lives in a patriarchal society where materialism and social hierarchies are everywhere. One example is that a contemporary Korean woman also carries the burden of finding a spouse whose economic and social status is higher than her own, because she is expected to be defined by her husband and his social and business success. And to do this, not only does a Korean woman have to be excellent at her job, she must also strive to live up to impossible standards set by a Korean lifestyle, which includes attaining Western ideals of beauty that have been influenced by post-colonial standards. So whether with regard to physical appearance, professional aptitude, or economic status, these examples show the ways in which Korean women live in the *han*-ridden culture that is plagued by materialism, patriarchy, and post-colonialism.

Especially in dealing with oppression of women in Korean culture, the influence of *han* cannot be ignored in the spirituality of contemporary Korean women. Andrew Sung Park explains that *han* is the experience of "crushing oppression and consequent suffering of people of low status," who are called *minjung*, because of their "daily terrors of want, powerlessness and subjugation."[7] Park argues that *han* manifests itself as a deep "inner wound" in Korean people's souls and is expressed as a "frustrated hope, a collapsed feeling of pain, a resentful bitterness, and a wounded heart."[8] Consequently, regardless of education and career success, contemporary Korean women, like *minjung*, continue to struggle with their low self-esteem caused by both gender discrimination and by a Western standard of physical appearance and concept of beauty. For that reason, whether Korean women acknowledge it or not, they live under the ideological oppression of a Korean

6. "South Korea Tops Plastic Surgery."
7. Park, *The Wounded Heart of God*, 52.
8. Ibid.

han-based culture that is shaped by contemporary patriarchal and postcolonial paradigms.

Christian women are no exception. The church conveniently does not help a Korean woman understand how herself, others, and churches are intertwined with the Korean *han* culture, instead insisting her virtue derives from following the expectations of this patriarchal church. For a woman to be virtuous, which Korean churches demand, she must be subservient to male hierarchy, just one compromise of combining the practices and systems of patriarchal Christianity and oppressive indigenous religions. Moreover, the Korean church historically has indoctrinated Korean women to believe that the true God is inherently, rather than by cultural convention, a patriarchal and oppressive God. The resultant hierarchical and oppressive church has capitalized on women's faithful piety and silence to make them expand the church and in so doing also expand patriarchy and oppression.

When, at some point, a Korean woman arrives at a realization of the oppressive power of the church, she tends to experience dissonance regarding what she should believe and how she should act. When she becomes aware that what the church, within its stained-glass box, has taught her is not actually the truth, she often has a spiritual crisis. Of course, the church does not help her understand her own feelings in that crisis. She begins to see the church, with its theology and value system, as being more oppressive than the society. Thus she feels increasingly depressed, discouraged, broken, and vulnerable.

Paradoxically, because she thinks of God as a liberator, she chooses to stay inactive in her mental captivity. She invokes her mighty God to help her by being faithful to her spiritual practices of fasting, prayers, reading the Bible, worship, commitment, and social services, which the church demands of her. But the more she tries, the more she realizes that she is only trying to constrain herself and her God within the glass box that the church has created. She does not know what to do; she finds herself on the border between the dual patriarchal oppressors: church and society. If she dares to evade the influence of the patriarchal *han*-ridden culture of the Korean church, she confronts strong resistance from both "men and women of God."[9] This leads her into conflicting situations that may make her an outcast of the system because she is challenging the existing value system of the church by attempting to escape its door-less, stained-glass box. Hampered by her strong fear and her ignorance, it is difficult for her to create a healthy image of God and herself, because she is constantly inundated with cultural messages that draw her back into the culture of *han*, both in the church and society.

To sum up, Christian women's experience of oppression in both the Korean church and culture must be examined together in order to create the awareness necessary for further steps in the liberation of Korean women. Elizabeth Condé-Frazier, in her essay "From Hospitality to Shalom," provides a theoretical foundation for the dynamics of culture and oppression in the faith system. As Condé-Frazier points out, "culture has been defined as the total pattern of a people's behavior that is learned and transmitted by the symbols (language, rights, and artifacts) of a particular group."[10] According to her, "these symbols focus on certain ideas or assumptions that become a worldview," because "culture expresses the values and purposes of each community as well as its sensitivities and spirituality."[11] As she argues, it is therefore important for both Korean women and men to know that "throughout history the church has taken different positions on the relationship between faith and culture. What stands in the midst of these diversities is the acceptance that faith is transmitted in cultural forms."[12] Accordingly, an oppressive culture is also manifested in faith system to produce another culture of oppression in Korean churches, especially against women.

For this reason, several scholars suggest that for an oppressed Korean woman to experience liberation she must awake from her

---

9. "Men and women of God" is normally used to express "sisters and brothers in Christ" among Christians.

10. Condé-Frazier, "From Hospitality to Shalom," 167.

11. Ibid.

12. Ibid., 168.

Introduction

ignorance of the *han*-based culture. Awaking from ignorance is the stage at which a woman finally becomes aware that she is in an invisible glass box. Then, the dark glass box becomes transparent thanks to this awareness. Anthony De Mello says "most people, even though they don't know it, are asleep."[13] The churches and religious systems "are unanimous on one thing: that all is well" they insist that "though everything is a mess, all is well"[14] to justify their oppression of women. However, as De Mello expresses, "tragically, most people never get to see that all is well because they are asleep. They are having a nightmare."[15] Both Korean women and men need to wake up to the perilous reality of the *han*-based oppressive Korean culture since they cannot isolate themselves from culture. In line with De Mello, the waking-up process of gaining awareness within an oppressive culture is a highly important stage of spirituality for Korean women.

This awareness process is sometimes referred to as "conscientization,"[16] a term that derives from the pedagogical and political research of Paulo Freire.[17] Conscientization is a learning process that empowers people's consciousness, makes them more critically aware of their social reality, gives them a dialogical consciousness, and enables them to see the possibility of their liberation. Conscientization is practiced in many countries, although notably in South America, and is based on trust in the lived experience of the oppressed and on leaders who are committed to both learning and educating through questioning and dialogue.[18]

To describe the conscientization process of Korean Christian women, I focus on the personal transformation of Korean women as they acquire a healthy sense of themselves through it,

13. De Mello, *Awareness*, 5.
14. Ibid.
15. Ibid.
16. The Spanish *concientización* is translated into English as either concientization or consientisation. It conveys the idea of developing, strengthening, and changing consciousness.
17. Paulo Freire, *Pedagogy of the Oppressed*.
18. Freire Institute, "Conscientization."

and on how this is a stepping stone to social transformation. This conscientization process I identify with Robert Clinton's term of "ministry out of being."[19] Ministry out of being means that as a woman gets to know herself and others in her culture—in short, as she becomes conscientized—her spirituality will bring about not only her personal transformation but will also contribute to a larger social transformation. Conscientization is therefore not only a protest but also a means of personal transformation. Such transformation leads to changes in relational patterns with other people and changes in a woman's social status in Korean culture.

As part of the conscientization process of Korean women, I explore the concept of *jeong*, which is the flipside of *han*. In Korean culture, the term *jeong* has multiple meanings, including the concepts of caring, loving, relationality, feeling, sentiment, sympathy, bonding, compassion, bondage, emotional attachment, and so on. I explore the comprehensive meanings of *jeong* as "affection,"[20] which can be a source of healing for Korean women, because the problems of *han* in Korean culture can be solved by the positive side of *jeong*. Just as Gerald May argues that "fear and desire are two sides of the same psychological coin,"[21] I understand *han* and *jeong* to function in much the same way. *Han* and *jeong* saturate daily living and all forms of relationships within the Korean context. Accordingly, since *han* is inevitably interwoven with the presence of *jeong* among Koreans, *jeong* and *han* are strongly interrelated at the heart of interpersonal relationships of Korean women because

---

19. Clinton, "Life Long Development."

20. According to Wikipedia, "affection" is: "disposition or rare state of mind or body that is often associated with a feeling or type of love. It has given rise to a number of branches of philosophy and psychology concerning emotion, disease, influence, state of being. 'Affection' is popularly used to denote a feeling or type of love, amounting to more than goodwill or friendship. Writers on ethics generally use the word to refer to distinct states of feeling, both lasting and spasmodic."
Joh, *Heart of the Cross*, 146.

21. May, *Will and Spirit*, 214.

Introduction

the root of the Chinese characters of both words come from the word for "human heart" or center of human being.²²

By understanding the dynamics of *han* and *jeong*, I believe both can be useful resources for healing of oppressed Korean women in a positive manner. Wonhee Anne Joh suggests that *jeong* alleviates the *han* of victimized Korean women by shaping networks that not only allow them to "survive brutal victimization, but also enable them to form solidarities that allow for the creation of movements to confront and resist various manifestations of violence."²³ Because the most dangerous thing for oppressed people is to become anesthetized through internalizing unfamiliar criteria and ignoring their own gut-feelings, Wonhee Anne Joh recommends that they permit themselves to fully experience who they are by creating their own space to meet God.²⁴ Oppressed Korean women need special places where they can be empowered and liberated and where the *jeong* of Korean women can be manifested in a positive way. For example, women can experience healings in the *jeong*-filled hospitality group of women, empowered by the sense of acceptance and belonging, when they feel vulnerable in an oppressive culture.

Because *jeong* can be a true spiritual construct for praxis, *jeong* manifests a Korean woman's core spirituality of hospitality. *Jeong* has great potential to be a "more powerful, lasting, and transformative energy than love," because of its characteristics of compassion, affection, solidarity, vulnerability, and forgiveness.²⁵

---

22. Much of Korean language uses the Chinese meanings. The Korean language 한 (*Han*) and 정 (*Jeong*) is transliterated from Chinese terms of 恨 and 情. The Chinese characters of *han* 恨 (한), and *jeong* 情 (정) contains the symbol of human hearts (心/忄). It is amazing to analyze *han* (한) in Chinese character of 恨 (resentment), with combination of 心, 日, 女 (heart, day [sun], woman). *Jeong* (정) has Chinese character of 情 (affection) with combination of 心, 手, 一, 月 (heart, hand, one, moon). Both have heart. Sun refers to man and moon refers to woman.

23. Joh, *Heart of the Cross*, 147.

24. Chung, "Han-pu-ri," 53.

25. Joh, *Heart of the Cross*, 146.

9

However, it also has its "sticky"[26] features, which can have the negative effect of intruding upon other people's emotional and spiritual boundaries. Notwithstanding, the properly balanced *jeong* can help Korean women to create a healthier image of self, others, and of society in God. I am convinced the healthy functioning of *jeong* in Korean culture can bring about a transformation of women, and allow them to begin reconciling the interpersonal conflicts that have been caused by the *han*-ridden culture of Korea.

As a first step in overcoming the oppression of contemporary Korean Christian women, I will propose several things the Korean church can do to reduce that oppression, because the church is a major part of the problem. My first recommendation is that we understand both *han*-ridden and *jeong*-filled Korean culture in the process of feminist "consciousness-raising"[27] as a way to articulate Korean women's God-experiences from both traditional and feminist perspectives. Because the *han* of women is the foundation of all Korean sub-consciousness due to the shameful history of the culture's inhumane treatment of women, a feminist theological analysis of Korean culture and society will liberate ordinary Korean women by showing them how to critically evaluate their current cultural roles and positions as oppressive. For this, I aim to critique the oppressive aspects of the *han*-ridden culture that have resulted in the marginalization of women in both past and present Korean society.

As a second step, I will explore a process of conscientization in which forgiveness and the praxis of true reconciliation provide

26. Ibid.

27. According to Wikipedia, "consciousness raising" is also called "awareness raising." The site describes consciousness raising as follows: "a form of political activism, popularized by United States feminists in the late 1960s. It often takes the form of a group of people attempting to focus the attention of a wider group of people on some cause or condition. Common issues include diseases (e.g. breast cancer, AIDS), conflicts (e.g. the Darfur genocide, global warming), movements (e.g. Greenpeace, PETA, Earth Hour), and political parties or politicians. Since informing the populace of a public concern is often regarded as the first step to changing how the institutions handle it, raising awareness is often the first activity in which any advocacy group engages." http://en.wikipedia.org/wiki/Consciousness_raising.

Introduction

stepping-stones for the social healing of Korea, and will help facilitate the spiritual formation of Korean Christian women through their reconstruction of a healthier self-image in God, Christ, the Christian community, and Korean society. Accordingly, I will explore the dynamics of conflict and reconciliation from theoretical and theological perspectives in the socio-cultural-religio context of Korean women, and analyze conscientization as a method of consciousness-raising. To aid in this exploration, I examine *Pedagogy of the Oppressed* by Paulo Freire in light of spiritual formation as well as feminist theologies. I also explore feminist perspectives on the practices of self-compassion, of the Internal Family System (IFS), and the contemplative methods of awareness.[28]

To this end, I accentuate the significance of spiritual formation in interpersonal conflicts and reconciliation of women in Korean culture, because I believe conflict situations can greatly shape the spirituality of women. I understand that a Korean woman's effort to understand the conflict as a way of spiritual formation will help her learn about "the holistic nature of spirituality,"[29] which will liberate her from the oppressive cultures of patriarchy and materialism in the context of post-colonialism. Mary John Mananzan and Sun Ai Park articulate the holistic nature of spirituality by saying: "When one is concerned with one's own stomach, it is materialism, but when one is concerned with the other people's stomachs, it is spirituality."[30]

Both are concerned with stomach, but one is called materialism and the other spirituality. Christian spirituality deals with this fine distinction, which can be summed up as the unity of self and others, the material and the spiritual, love and justice, community and individuals, religions and politics, peace and struggle toward holistic salvation. Women's struggle is part and parcel of the historical struggle for the holistic salvation of all humanity. Women

---

28. I got this idea from my Spiritual Formation for Compassionate Social Engagement class, lectured by Frank Rogers at Claremont School of Theology in Claremont, California (fall semester 2011).

29. Mananzan and Park, "Emerging Spirituality," 78.

30. Ibid.

can make a unique contribution toward this goal based on their concrete pro-life way of living and experiences. All the disastrous dimension of patriarchal culture is typically exemplified in its demeaning, ignoring, and despising the very spirituality of women that is oriented toward and sustaining life in love.[31]

Mananzan and Park write of the spirituality of women as affirming womanhood because it interacts with the world in a way that is for "liberating all women and all humanity."[32] They suggest that a woman who is discriminated against for being a woman needs to fight for a powerful position within the oppressive culture by radically bringing about "values that are people-oriented concerned for life and for a truly humane community."[33] They highlight the goal of this movement with the following message: "This goal is a double task for a better society with women leaders. But if we women claim to be the hope, we must carry out this task. There is no easy way out."[34]

My argument proceeds as follows: in chapter 2, I showcase the interpersonal conflicts of Korean women in what I have earlier called the invisible (dark) glass box. I will contextualize the diverse ways that Korean women experience oppression in traditional families and contemporary socio-cultural-historical-religious spiritual contexts. Insights in this section reflect my personal narrative of oppression in Korean culture and churches. In chapter 3, I portray conscientization and Korean women's awareness of oppression as the stage of a visible glass box. I will provide a theoretical background of the oppressive and liberative dynamics of *han* and *jeong* in Korean culture, supported by the conscientization process, feminist theology, and third-world feminist theology in light of the dynamics of *han* and *jeong*, and Korean women's experiences of interpersonal conflicts in Korean culture, including the narrative of my personal journey/struggle to break the glass box.

31. Ibid.
32. Ibid.
33. Ibid.
34. Ibid.

Introduction

In chapter 4, I show how Korean women can break the glass box by applying contemplative practices of conscientization, which include a liberation process of re-imaging self and God. I examine the Internal Family System (IFS) and "compassion practices" as means by which Korean women can build healthy self-images that will lead to their personal and social transformation. I then apply these practices to the theological and pedagogical implication of Paulo Freire's theory of conscientization.

In chapter 5, I propose a Korean women's *jeong*-oriented spirituality as a new cultural paradigm for breaking the glass box. The chapter moves from conscientization to reconciliation for Korean women by examining the characteristics of a *jeong*-filled praxis of hospitality as a holistic Korean women's spirituality. I will use the metaphor of sticky rice as a powerful image of a *jeong*-filled solidarity group as a new paradigm for liberating Korean women.

Chapter 2

The Invisible Glass Box
Interpersonal Conflicts of Korean Women

Oppressive Conditions of Korean Women in Socio-Historical Contexts

Traditional Familial Contexts

THIS CHAPTER EXAMINES KOREAN women's experiences of oppression in traditional family contexts. An old Korean saying reflects the challenges contemporary Korean women face in their search to be liberated from male-centered norms both in Korean culture and churches. It states, "Three men determine the fate of every woman, and they are her father, her husband, and her son."[1] For me, this saying embodies the metaphor of the invisible glass box that is the root cause of interpersonal conflicts Korean women experience in all aspects of Korean life and culture. With a woman's fate resting in the hands of the men in her family, Choi Hee An notes that a Korean woman cannot be a protagonist in her own life but is only the "other" who "never belongs to her family."[2]

1. Schroeder, Review of *Korean Women*.
2. Choi, *Korean Women And God*, 56.

The Invisible Glass Box

Traditional Korean family systems based on Confucianist principles still today define a Korean woman's identity and existence in relationship to men in her roles as a daughter, daughter-in-law, wife, and mother further solidify this sense of fate. Consequently, until recently anonymity has been the norm for women in Korean culture; for example, often their names refer them as someone's daughter, wife, or mother, but never as simply themselves. A Korean woman only becomes "an insider" and "a person of status" by being a loyal wife and daughter-in-law.[3] Thus, a Korean woman's status and survival in her family depends on male relationships that include marriage and her ability to give birth to a son or sons in order to continue the family name. For centuries, Confucian-based patriarchy has solidified this ideological construct in family structures that have given women no respect as unmarried, widowed, separated, divorced, barren, or single mothers, but only as good wives and wise mothers.[4] Women who deviated from these prescribed norms, roles, and responsibilities lost their place and social status in their families and society.[5]

Because of these rigidly defined social roles, Korean women tended to be trapped within the socio-cultural and invisible glass boxes of prescribed roles and responsibilities for them as daughters, wives, and mothers, roles that led to conflicting relationships within themselves and with others in their families and society. Choi Hee An writes of how Korean women were taught to sacrifice themselves for others and to deny their own needs for the noble causes of both their husbands' family and society.[6] Until modernity, women have been traditionally excluded from educational and social systems and have not been deemed valuable and autonomous beings in their own right.

Furthermore, a Korean woman in a traditional family context was expected to sacrifice her life for her family and to be subordinate to men, something she manifested by her quietness,

3. Ibid., 150.
4. Ibid., 58.
5. Ibid., 150.
6. Ibid., 4.

submission, and obedience. It was only in relationship to a man or men that she had any meaning, identity, and place in society. Unsurprisingly, Korean women's understandable fears and their desire to be accepted as "insiders" for their own survival has caused them to be too anxiously attached to their children, burdening their sons with high expectations and their daughters with their own frustrations. Mothers tend to see the *han* of their own lives mirrored in the lives of their daughters, creating mixed feelings of both anger and compassion toward their suffering and that of other Korean women. The title of John Sweeney's book, *I'd Rather Dead Than Be a Girl*, also echoes this invisibility and despairs of women in Korean society.[7]

It is an unjust situation that has led Korean women to accumulate centuries of *han*. Although women have traditionally been responsible for managing the household finances in such a way as to provide for their husbands' and children's needs, they have not been allowed to express their feelings and struggles openly in any context. Consequently, Korean women have vented their unresolved *han* of "defeat, resignation, the tenacity of life, or grudges"[8] mainly in their relationships with other women, that is, between mother-in-laws and daughter-in-laws, sisters-in-law, mothers and daughters, and even among daughters in their own households.

The psychological dynamics of oppression connected with *han* have created a vicious cycle between Korean women: a mother-in-law who herself is a victim of oppression becomes the oppressor of her daughter-in-law, and the cycle continues. Some pioneering Korean feminist theologians such as Chung Hyun Kyung have made great contributions in theology by discovering, naming, claiming, and creating the *han*-ridden history of Korean women. Asian American feminist theologians such as Kwok Pui-lan and Rita Nakashima Brock challenge us to think about how Korean women have suffered "with regard to the impact of colonialism on their culture, multiplicity and hybridity," and of how

---

7. Sweeney, *I'd Rather Be Dead*, 5.
8. Suh, "Toward a Theology of Han," 58.

The Invisible Glass Box

the popular religions of Korea have shaped women's lives in both past and present Korean society.[9]

Historical-Religio-Spiritual Contexts

In this section, I explore the historical background of the *han*-ridden religio-spiritual contexts in which Korean women have endured in the four major religions of Korea, that is, in Shamanism, Buddhism, Confucianism, and Christianity. I have found that because a wide variety of religious elements have shaped the worldview, behavior, and spirituality of Koreans, they typically do not differentiate between the religious and political spheres of life. In modern times, Christianity has made strong inroads into Korea and has in turn further shaped the spiritual and religious landscape for Korean men and women.[10] Historically, the spirituality of Korean Christian women has been shaped under the influences of Shamanism, Buddhism, and Confucianism.

Choi Hee An argues that since all four major religions tended to articulate a male-oriented ideology, regardless of the obvious ubiquity of Korean women's experiences, it is important to explore how Korean women's understanding of God has been a factor in their oppression over the centuries.[11] Because Korea's "theological context was larger than the religio-cultural sphere,"[12] as Chung Hyun Kyung argues, it is also important for me as a Christian woman to explore how the three historical religions have influenced Christianity as it was integrated into Korean culture.

Shamanism

Historically, shamanism is one of the oldest indigenous religions in Korea. It is estimated to have existed in Korea from at least the

---

9. Puil-lan, "Fishing the Asian Pacific," 10.
10. "Historical and Modern Religions of Korea."
11. Choi, *Korean Women*, 6.
12. Chung, *Struggle to be the Sun Again*, 13.

tenth century B.C.E.[13] Korean shamanism introduced polytheistic and animistic concepts into the agrarian culture of ancient Korea,[14] affirming different gods in the form of animals, plants, wind, agriculture, longevity, water, and rain. Presumably, this was a response to people's needs to drive away calamities and to invite blessings that included myths and folktales of strong women and goddesses who were dear to the daily lives of ordinary Korean women and men.[15] Choi Man Ja suggests that in Korea, "the pulse of the Korean people's mind beats through shamanism."[16] She asserts that shamanistic faith or customs are the most pervasive form of religious culture in Korea and that shamanistic rituals known as *kut* express the very soul and essence of the Korean *minjung* (common people) and their culture.[17] She adds that through the ages ordinary people have culturally transmitted the aspects of Korean shamanism owing to their relationship with their shaman priests known as *mudang*.

One of the most important characteristics of Korean shamanism was that it represented the voices of oppressed peoples, especially women,[18] because it had no hierarchy, no institutional body, and no doctrine. Instead, what became important was the ritual of "Han-pu-ri," which includes spiritual exorcism, direct communication with the spirits, and healing through the *mudang*,[19] a Korean shaman who played the role of the priest/ess of Han-pu-ri in his or her communities."[20] Through *kut*, a ritual of Shamanism, and storytelling, women were able to release their accumulated suffering of *han*. We see a great deal of evidence of the strong interconnection of Korean women's lives with the daily practice of shamanistic rituals. For instance, in the southern part of Korea, the

13. Choi, *Korean Women and God*, 11.
14. Choi, "Feminist Images," 82.
15. Ibid., 88.
16. Ibid., 81.
17. Ibid.
18. Choi, *Korean Women*, 17.
19. Choi, "Feminist Images," 82.
20. Chung, *"Han-pu-ri,"* 143.

first thing women usually do after daybreak is to show reverence to the gods as "protectors and benefactors"[21] by offering a bowl of pure water at the kitchen altar.[22]

Unfortunately, Korean women devoted themselves to these gods in a manner similar to the ways they worshipped their human "protectors" who were often colonizers and oppressors.[23] Choi Hee An notes that Korean women think of themselves as "not good enough" to please their gods and presumably by extension others in power, including men, regarding themselves as powerless people who must cede control to a higher power in order to be protected.[24] Further, Choi notes that Korean shamanism has put Korean women in danger of permanently losing their own sources of strength because of unhealthy images they have of gods who are ungenerous, angry, and irritable, "similar to the human beings who are supposed to be women's protectors."[25]

Additionally, in contemporary Korean society, female shamans who have spiritual power have been regarded as "polluting, dangerous, mystical, and unclean," because they used to be socially marginalized people who were a part of the lowest class in the Confucianistic hierarchy during the Chosun Dynasty.[26] Until the nineteenth century, shamanism was regarded as the superstitious spiritual practice of uneducated women and the poor and was driven underground with the coming of Christianity.[27] However, according to Choi Hee An, regardless of cultural prejudices and the marginalization of shamanism in modern society, shamanism has provided an array of diverse understandings of God to the *minjung* of Korea. That these images arise from their authentic lives and are

21. Choi, *Korean Women*, 15.
22. Ibid., 13.
23. Ibid., 15.
24. Ibid.
25. Ibid.
26. Ibid., 17.
27. Ibid., 18.

centered on reconciliation and peace helps women to resist the oppressive *han*-ridden culture of colonialism and patriarchy.[28]

Buddhism

Buddhism, as a religious construct and ideology, had a significant impact on Korean mindsets as well as the national religion under the Three Kingdoms, Unified Silla, and Koryo Kingdom (918–1392 A.D.), which helped to shield the Korean nation from foreign countries.[29] Historically, it was necessary for Buddhism to adapt itself to Eastern philosophies in order to be adopted by native-born Koreans. Unlike shamanism, regardless of governmental efforts to support Buddhist monks and to build Buddhist temples and monasteries, Buddhism did not easily attract the common people.[30]

In this process of "Koreanization," Buddhism was integrated into shamanism in the service of national unity and defense.[31] Buddhist temples were made to look like shamanistic shrines where the people could pray and consult with the monks, whom they regarded as shamans. Because of this, Korean Buddhism embraced the divine images of shamanistic gods to attract the common people—especially women—who prayed every day even though Buddhism itself does not have a concept of a God or Supreme Being. Choi notes that Korean women do not have the same images of God in Shamanism as they did in Buddhism, but they have maintained a similar attitude of fidelity and loyalty in Buddhist practices as they had in their daily shamanistic devotions.[32]

Buddhism teaches that all beings are equal. It provides an "androgynous aspect"[33] of religion that allowed women to create

28. Ibid., 21–22.
29. Ibid., 24.
30. Ibid., 24–26.
31. Ibid., 26.
32. Ibid., 30.

33. According to Wikipedia, "Androgyny is a term derived from the Greek words ανήρ, stem ανδρ- (*anér, andr-*, meaning man) and γυνή (*gyné*, meaning woman), referring to the combination of masculine and feminine

images of female divine power. This, for women, transformed femininity into something in which they were able to escape their sufferings and see themselves as enlightened beings equal to men.[34] However, as Korean Buddhism became linked with hierarchal political structures and rituals led by male monks, women began to lose the ability to see themselves as equals. Additionally, in the Chosun Dynasty, shamanized Buddhism merged with Confucian ideologies, which were strongly grounded in patriarchal and hierarchal structures.[35] For more than five centuries, Korean women mutely maintained their faith and practice of shamanistic Buddhism under oppressive Confucianism and the Chosun Dynasty, as it was the only channel through which to release their *han*.

Confucianism

For five centuries, during the Chosun/Yi Dynasty (1392–1910), the principles of Confucianism dominated both the governmental and familial structures of the ruling Yi family. At that time, Confucianism was the only nationally legitimized religion. It replaced the previously powerful Buddhist elites of the Koryo Kingdom who were subsequently expelled from Korea. Originally, the principles of Confucianism placed a high value on order and harmony as described in the concepts of Yin and Yang, in which "heaven and earth exist as essentially life giving."[36] Accordingly, in Korean culture, Yin and Yang produced and reproduced all things in the universe through their interaction. Historically, this teaching was an important Confucian principle that encouraged respect for all life forms and laid the foundation for ancestor worship.[37]

Yin and Yang were not based on a hierarchical value system but were understood as dynamic principles and complementarities.

---

characteristics."
34. Choi, *Korean Women*, 31.
35. Ibid., 33.
36. Ibid., 36.
37. Kelleher, "Confucianism," 138–39.

It was only later in Korean history that Confucianism transformed the relationship of Yin and Yang into a coercive oppressive force for Korean women by stressing gender hierarchies rather than complementarities between these two forces. Thus, Confucian thought distorted the balance and positive energy between Yin and Yang that had, for centuries, "guided natural processes and human beings to a point of harmonious balance between extremes."[38]

Furthermore, Korean culture used a Confucian hierarchy to maintain a cosmic order in which heaven, husband, king, parents, and men were elevated to a higher position in contrast to the earth, wife, servant, children, and women whose status shifted to a lower position. This hierarchy demanded that people in lower positions be obedient to their superiors, and it further legitimized the power of men who in Korean culture have dominated those superior positions. Confucian ethics thus assumed dominance of women by men.

Historically, this religious tradition solidified sexist thinking in Korean culture, past and present. Sherry Orthner asserts that Confucian principles encourage a "universal devaluation of women based on a [the] cultural assumption of the hierarchy of culture over sin."[39] In Confucianism, there is no room for egalitarian relationships between men and women. Women are simply expected to follow male orders and fulfill their duty of producing a continuous male genealogy. In this ideological framework, only sons mattered, since they uniquely brought honor and glory to the family through official appointments and the passing on of the family name.[40] For that reason, Confucianism, as a religious ideology, exalts the authority of fathers and sons and makes the unequal treatment of women seem natural.[41] For instance, this institutionalized ethics and the women's *Three Virtues of Obedience*, *Sam-chong-ji-gui*, reinforced the images of the ideal woman who

---

38. Ingram, *Constructing a Relational Cosmology*, 8.
39. Park, *The Wounded Heart*, 52.
40. Kang, "Confucian Familism," 173.
41. Ibid., 174.

obeyed her parents in girlhood, her husband in marriage, and her sons in old age.[42]

In Korean history, further, Confucian teachings deeply influenced dualistic hierarchies in five basic types of human relationships: between king and minister, husband and wife, older and younger persons, men and women, and friends. For example, for thousands of years, the seven Eligible Grounds for Divorce in Confucian principles show the marginalized status of women. These assumptions or seven rules for a woman to avoid committing sins are:[43]

1) She must not be disobedient, in behavior, to her parents-in-law.

2) She must give birth to a son.

3) She should not be too talkative.

4) She shall not commit adultery.

5) She shall not be jealous of her husband's concubine.

6) She shall not carry a malignant disease.

7) She shall not commit theft.

These ideological mandates further solidified the imbalance and inequalities between Korean men and women on the basis of "a deontological ethic" that justified the inferiority of women to men, "by invoking a divine mandate," that Korean men were superior in nature to Korean women.[44] *Han*, an already oppressive force in Korean women's lives and intensified as Korean men, was elevated to a higher status as a result of Confucianism being "inevitability patriarchal, patrilineal, and patrilocal."[45] In contemporary Korea, however, most people continue to be strongly influenced by Confucian values in their daily lives, even though Confucian texts are seldom read and rituals associated with this religion either have been simplified or abandoned altogether.[46] To

42. Yi, "Christian Mission," 93.
43. Park, *The Wounded Heart*, 54.
44. Ibid.
45. Kang, "Confucian Familism," 174.
46. Ibid., 172.

date, in Korean culture, Confucianism is "the most biologically rooted [religion] of all human institutions."[47] This is so because it has been the official philosophy and religion of the Yi Dynasty dating to 1392–1910 in Korea.[48]

Family systems, in particular, show the strong influence of Confucianism because the family is "enshrined as a sacred community" and is "considered the natural basis for all moral and political behavior."[49] Thus, to this day Confucianism continues to be comprehensively institutionalized and systematically diffused in Korean culture.[50] Because of this strong influence of Confucianism in Korean society, Christianity, as a western religion in Korea, could not help developing its contextualized religiosity to the extent that Korean Christianity is considered "Confucianized Christianity."[51] Accordingly, Western modernization of Korea has also integrated colonial ideologies into Korean Confucianism, Buddhism, shamanistic cultures, and Christian traditions, thus strengthening patriarchal church systems in Korea.[52]

Christianity

Catholicism was the first form of Christianity introduced in Korea, one hundred years earlier than Protestantism. Christianity arrived in 1783 and was presented as a "Western Study," which explored "belief in the Christian God without the influence of colonial Western power."[53] However, as a part of the invasion of the American government beginning in 1875, both Catholic and Protestant Christianity began to perpetuate Western colonialism and Western ideologies in Korean society.[54] The task of Western

47. Ibid., 172–73.
48. Ibid., 172.
49. Ibid.
50. Ibid.
51. Ibid.
52. Choi, *Korean Women*, 40.
53. Ibid., 41.
54. Ibid.

The Invisible Glass Box

missionaries was not always easy, as they faced heavy resistance from indigenous Koreans, who saw Christianity as destroying the spirits of Korean people, because it disrespected Korean culture, people, society, and gods.[55] Because of its renunciation of traditional Korean culture, the first hundred years of Korean Christian history were full of stories about the martyrdom of missionaries who denounced ancestor worship and insisted on worship of the Christian God alone.

After the collapse of the Yi Dynasty, Protestant Christianity began to grow by bringing revolutionary changes into the lives of Korean people.[56] Koreans began to accept Christianity as a powerful moral force because it helped Koreans to achieve independence from Japanese colonization in Korea. Nevertheless, many other Korean religions still protested that Christianity was a Western colonial religion. To this day, this controversial issue of Christianity as a Western religion is the topic of an ongoing cultural discussion in Korea's postmodern society.[57]

As a result of the influence of the western Christianity, missionary and evangelical activities of Korean Christianity have concentrated on direct propagation of the gospel as well as creating educational and medical services for evangelical purposes. These efforts have proved extremely attractive to Korean women, who are the main source of Christianity's growth in Korea.[58] In tandem with the growing number of churches and revival prayer meetings, the role of female evangelists in churches increased and began to influence the "pattern of faith prevalent among women believers in the understanding of the Bible."[59] Instead of the oppressive *han* culture of the Yi Dynasty, Christianity provided women with hope for a new era of liberation and social change. It released women from the oppressive principles advocated by Confucianism, offering them opportunities to freely go outside the home, to partici-

---

55. Ibid., 42.
56. Yi, "Christian Mission," 93.
57. Choi, *Korean Women*, 43.
58. Yi, "Christian Mission," 94.
59. Ibid., 96.

pate in various activities in the church, as well as to pursue new educational opportunities.⁶⁰

However, as Christianity has become more fully integrated into Korean religions, Korean Christian women have found their faith in tension with conflicting dynamics of freedom and oppression in the church. They could not enjoy full liberation in Korean churches, regardless of the liberating message of the gospel of Jesus. Nonetheless, despite the oppressive aspects of the Korean churches, Korean women have contributed greatly to the growth of the Korean church simply by constituting the majority of most congregations. In contemporary Korean churches, though women constitute 70 percent of the population, "the institutions of the Korean church still remain patriarchal," because they refuse to allow women to hold high leadership positions in the church.⁶¹

In Korea, additionally, to live as a Christian, one is required to choose one direction only, which is to follow Western Christianity, since in Korean churches there is no respect for indigenous religions. In view of that, by naming them as demonic and thus a hindrance to her spiritual journey, the church encourages a Korean Christian woman only to resist the traditional Korean cultural and religious practices, and indeed it indoctrinates her to believe that the church is the only way to salvation. However, many values and practices of Korean Christianity have been shaped and contextualized under the *han*-based patriarchy reflective of the indigenous religions in Korea. Thus, most theological and ministerial practices in Korean churches, including its Bible study, preaching, worship, and pastoral care and counseling for the members of the congregation have also been shaped by the patriarchal and *han*-based natures of Korean religions, that is, Shamanism, Buddhism, and Confucianism. Particularly, for Christianity, as a Western religion in Korea, it is also clear that the Korean church has adopted Western patriarchy and materialism into the indigenous *han*-based patriarchy, uniting them under the umbrella of post-colonialism.

60. Choi, *Korean Women*, 44.
61. Yi, "Christian Mission," 102.

Oppressive Conditions for Korean Women in Contemporary Society

Contemporary Paradigms for Korean Women's Role in Family, Education, and Employment

Since the 1960s, South Korea has experienced astonishing economic growth through modernization, industrialization, urbanization, and globalization. The changes continue, and indeed, since overcoming the International Monetary Fund (IMF) economic crisis of 1997, Korean society has undergone faster and bigger transitions in culture, value systems, and life styles, moving toward a more individualistic and materialistic society that values independence. The traditional sense of family has been abandoned with the spread of individualism, since "individualism and independence are the antithesis of familism,"[62] and with it also the traditional sense of education and employment.

First, the underlying shift in the Korean family system has prompted all the other changes. Unlike the Confucian-based traditional family structure, the contemporary South Korean family structure is nuclear, the result of industrialization in the 1960s and 1970s.[63] Because of modernization and urbanization, younger generations are leaving their rural hometowns to live in cities where they can pursue higher education and a greater variety of employment opportunities. Such movement has split up large families that traditionally had lived closer together. As a result, contemporary Korean families and culture have become more individualistic and independent, the antithesis of the traditional familism[64] based on patriarchal Confucianism. Divorce, which in Confucian society only happened through abjection by the husband or the husband's family, is now occurring far more often as a result of changing attitudes of Korean women toward marriage, childbearing, and cohabitation, and underlying all these, their

---

62. Han, "Tradition and Modernity," 44.
63. "Changes of the Family System in Korea."
64. Choi, "The Impact of Industrialization," 114.

newfound economic independence.⁶⁵ Clearly, the transformation of the Korean family value system has greatly altered women's roles both in the family and in society.

Second, there has been a big change in the education of women in Korea. In traditional Korean society, women received little formal education. During early economic development in 1960s and 1970s, girls were supposed to support their brothers' educations. With the advent of the nuclear family due partly to the Korean government's policy encouraging families to have only one or two children in the early 1970s, however, women began to have more educational opportunities. By 1987, there were ten institutions of higher education for women—including universities, colleges, and junior colleges—and women accounted for approximately 28 percent of total enrollment in higher education.⁶⁶ By 2012, Korean women were earning five times as many advanced degrees as they were in 1995.

These changes have been so rapid and pervasive that today it is possible to say that there is no gender discrimination in the current Korean education system. In general, universities and employers are basing their enrollment and hiring practices more and more on merit and less on gender. As economic development progressed, the living conditions of Koreans improved, and women's level of education increased, they began to engage in the arts, teaching, and various other professional careers.⁶⁷ This has had the effect of upgrading women's social status, as South Korea has become the "ideal environment for gender arbitrage."⁶⁸

Third, the social participation of women through jobs has increased with modernization. Whereas in the past traditional women's roles confined them to the home, and whereas, in 1975 only 2 percent of the female labor force worked in professional or managerial occupations, and 4 percent in clerical positions,⁶⁹ by

65. "Marriage in South Korea."
66. "Women in South Korea."
67. "Women's Role in Contemporary Korea."
68. "Profiting from Sexism."
69. "Women's Role in Cotemporary Korea."

The Invisible Glass Box

1998 12.6 percent of female employees were serving in professional or managerial positions, and another 16 percent were working in clerical occupations. With an increasing number of women entering professional jobs, in 1987 the government passed the Equal Employment Act to prevent discriminatory hiring and promotion practices against female workers.[70] Visibly and statistically, Korean women of today are actively engaged in a wide variety of fields, including education, medicine, engineering, scholarship, the arts, law, literature, and sports.

Sexism, Oppression, and Women's Experiences in Contemporary Korean Society

In the above section, we saw how the new paradigm for Korean women's roles in family, education, and employment coincided with the rapid economic development of contemporary Korean society. Since women's roles have changed so rapidly, especially with the development of the nuclear family system, Korean women of the twenty-first century find it difficult to value traditional roles. However, regardless of statistics that show women's improving social status, in reality Korean women still experience inequality with Korean men in the workplace; their gender is still "a handicap."[71]

As in many countries in the world, since patriarchy is defined in terms of power and ideology, men in Korea obviously possess superior social, cultural, and economic power. Under a patriarchal power structure reinforced by an underlying ideology of men's superiority, we notice the "subordination of women" in their unequal access to employment opportunities and in particular to senior positions, as well as in the male-dominated culture and language.[72] Ji-Sun Chung writes regarding this reality of Korean women's careers:

70. Ibid.
71. Lee, *The Meaning*, 56.
72. Jung, "Women's Unequal Access," 487.

> The basic proposition of such theories is that capitalist economic development and patriarchy interact to subordinate women. While capitalist development reinforces women's economic oppression by utilizing them primarily as cheap labor, patriarchal ideology views women as inferior and expects them to function only as homemakers and mothers. Accordingly, less emphasis is placed for women on education or high occupational attainment, which are reserved for men. Conflicts over the exploitation of women's labor between patriarchal and capitalist interests are endemic to the history of the interaction between the two systems.[73]

Thus, while contemporary Korean women may not consciously recognize gender discrimination since gender equality in the educational system has begun to be enforced in the past few decades, Korean women, nonetheless, endure oppression under a male-oriented culture. The result is often women at conflict with themselves and others as they try to fulfill their dreams in Korean society. Consciously and subconsciously, because of their gender-biased culture, Korean women are persuaded that they are somehow deficient or inferior to men. For instance, many Korean women abandon their careers when they get married or have children; often such "career interruptions" push them to accept decreased wages, depreciation of their skills, or even complete loss of their professional careers.[74] The Korean cultural assumption that "the mother's first duty is to raise the child, and no one else can substitute for the mother" pushes career women to leave their careers when they get married or pregnant.[75] Cultural expectations tend to make them feel guilty for assigning the care of their children to others, and so they quit their professions instead.

Connie Chung argues that even for the most trivial reasons social segregation on the basis of gender reinforces the status of men as being more valuable than women.[76] This bias is rooted in

73. Ibid.
74. Lee, *The Meaning*, 4.
75. "Women's Role in Contemporary Korea."
76. Chung, "Korean Society and Women."

The Invisible Glass Box

the social norm that men and women are inherently different in character and ability, a distinction that favors men by defining women as the "weaker sex of the species."[77] According to this bias, men are inherently wiser, more courageous, tenacious, cool-headed, reasonable, and born leaders, while women are considered inherently more prudent, selfless, patient, sensitive, emotional, and irrational. This gender segregation sets up a strict dichotomy between the sexes, teaching that each sex possesses the qualities of one category but not the other.[78]

I have experienced that such ideology is deeply ingrained in both women and men, and functions to repress women in Korean society. Typically, Korean women will not understand why they cannot escape from gender discrimination until they become aware of the ingrained and oppressive patriarchal social structures in Korean culture and structures based on Confucian and Buddhist traditions as well as on the capitalist economic mentality that emerged during post-colonialism. Along with living in an invisible "glass box" without doors, Korean women must endure invisible "glass partitions"[79] in Korean culture and society. Both the invisible glass box and partition confine Korean women into certain gendered, cultural norms—even in twenty-first-century society. The glass box and glass partitions are composed of historical and inherited *han*-based principles that have evolved in Korean culture.

Sexism, Oppression, and Women in Korean Churches

In response to modernization and the spread of western Christianity, South Korea began to recognize the need to educate women. This happened in the midst of colonialism and post-colonialism, when "Koreans accepted western civilization in order to strengthen

---

77. Ibid.
78. Ibid.
79. Lee, *The Meaning*, 56.

national power and attempted to develop their resources of people power through education for both sexes."[80] However, even as such education occurred, Korean Christian churches became another source of oppression of women, as the church prohibited women from holding positions of authority and leadership in the church.

Historically, Korean Christianity has been established "on top of" the indigenous Korean religions of Shamanism, Buddhism, and Confucianism. In particular, the influence of the patriachical and hierarchical structure of Confucianism has deepened the sexual discrimination in church structures, something that has not been voiced openly by Korean women until recently. Regardless of their seminary education, equally with men, but unlike men, women could not be ordained as pastors in most denominations and churches. Additionally, it has not been easy for women to have the ministry opportunities in the local Korean churches. Unlike men, women ministers could not be senior pastors of local churches nor have chances to preach on Sunday services. The salaries for female pastors have been lower than those of male pastors. They could find their voices only when they became missionaries in the poor countries or served in isolated places where no male pastors worked in Korea.

Adopting the western understanding of God, Korean Christianity acknowledged that Korea's national sins were the result of the traditional Confucian worship of ancestors and of Buddhist and Shamanist worship of pantheistic gods. Yi Hyo-Jae observes that the characteristic of faith for Korean Christian women is "an acknowledgement of the sins of the nation and each individual, a desire to be blessed by peace of mind and grace of spirit, [and] the ability to endure any difficulty in this world so that everyone may be saved in the next life."[81] As Yi Hyo-Jae asserts, Korean churches remain largely a community of an other-worldly faith in Korean society, believing and hoping for a better life in the next world.[82] In agreement with Yi Hyo-Jae, I maintain that the spirituality of well-

80. Yi, *Christian Mission*, 102.
81. Ibid.
82. Ibid., 101.

The Invisible Glass Box

being for individual Christian women has been ignored because the purpose and method of women's evangelical work have tended to remain on the level at which the gospel focused on a Korean style of communal faith, specifically on "the individual salvation and eschatological salvation of human kind for the solution of national affairs."[83]

This has happened mostly through the commitment to prayers and a willingness to sacrifice a person's life for the political liberation of Korea from colonial and post-colonial oppressors. Thus, the organization and the relationships of the Korean church remain an extension of patriarchal authority, a "reflection of materialism accompanied by modernization, social inequality, [and] undemocratic family life,"[84] which demands women be dominated by men. However, because Christianity has been heavily influenced by patriarchal traditions in Korean culture and has reinforced the legacy of post-colonialism, particular attributes of God that Korean women ascribe to have continued to foster the patriarchal system of the church, which oppresses women and sacrifices them. Even though Korean women have become more and more educated, gender equality has not been attained in the Korean church community.[85]

Yet, because Korean Christianity has been credited with revolutionary changes in the lives of Korean women, a re-evaluation both of the status and roles of women within the Korean church should be undertaken.[86] According to Park Sun-Kyung, "church women, who constitute as much as seventy percent of the Christian population of Korea, do not share proportionately in the operations of the Korean church."[87] It confines women to the "stained-glass box with a stained-glass ceiling"[88] of their Christian

83. Ibid., 102.
84. Ibid.
85. Ibid., 101.
86. Ibid., 93.
87. Ibid.
88. I coin this term to express the hierarchal characteristics of the Korean church.

faith instead of liberating them personally and socio-culturally as the liberating gospel of Jesus Christ is supposed to do. These boxes are reinforced by the inherited *han*-based culture of Korea.

Before I move on to discussing the transparency of the glass box, I will portray my experiences of Korean women's oppression in Korean churches.

A Personal Narrative of Sexism in Korean Churches

When I made a decision to be a pastor in my early thirties, it was not easy for me to respond to God's call. Not only did it not conform to the life trajectory I had laid out for myself since childhood, it also brought with it a set of new challenges because few women in Korean churches have been ordained and most of them are not respected by their male counterparts and Korean congregants. Thus, creating and projecting positive images of a female pastor in Korean churches has been difficult since only male pastors were granted automatic respect. Also, it was not easy for me to imagine myself in a leadership position as a senior pastor in a male-dominated Korean church because it was difficult to find good female role models.

I have observed that most Korean female pastors fit into one of three categories. First, there are unmarried female evangelists who assist male pastors in Korean mega-churches. Second, there are ordained female pastors who cultivate a masculine image by acting and talking like men. Third and last, there are the more charismatic female pastors who act much like shamans, but they were also despised and shunned by most Koreans. Some of them operated their own churches, but these were usually in out-of-the-way places in the mountains, because these pastors could not use their charismatic gifts in the structured and mainline churches of Korea.

Given all this, I was very hesitant to enter a seminary. Doing so meant being a full-time pastor who lived like Jesus and the Apostle Paul, a person who was willing to sacrifice her life for God. I assumed that once I entered seminary I would live as an ordained

The Invisible Glass Box

pastor without doing any secular work. But I did not want to cut myself off from secular life if the best I could hope for was to be relegated to assisting a male pastor, or to be forced to abandon my femininity and cultivate masculine characteristics, or to be shunned for being too "shamanistic."

After much discernment and a surrendering process, I finally decided to reclaim my agency and work toward being ordained in a knowingly patriarchal Korean culture and church. In my case, it also took a long time for me to find a seminary that supported the ordination of female pastors. Eventually, I entered a master's of divinity program in the United States, thinking it would be easier to be ordained in the United States than in Korea. I assumed that I would be ordained within a few years of graduating from a U.S. seminary. But I was wrong about that.

Upon graduation, I was interviewed for a position as a children's pastor at a big Korean American church located in Los Angeles. At that time, I asked the male Korean pastor who interviewed me, "What do you think about Korean women being ordained pastors?" He replied:

> I think female pastors in Korean churches are often miserable because they are regarded as inferior to male pastors regardless of their education. Some of them actually have better ministerial abilities than their male counterparts but they go unacknowledged because of their gender. Their salaries are lower than those of male pastors. They cannot be ordained and respected like male pastors in our church. In fact, my church ordains women as pastors only on the condition that they go to third-world countries as missionaries.[89]

He concluded by saying that he would not hire me because I was a woman and thus he could not trust me. His unabashed sexism crushed my spirit. I left the interview distressed.

In retrospect, I intended to stay in the dark glass box, because I did not want to believe that the majority of Christian Korean

---

89. These sentences are an excerpt from the conversation with the pastor during the job interview. I would like to leave his name anonymous.

churches held the opinion of this Korean male pastor. I thought that perhaps this male cleric's opinion of female ordination did not reflect the viewpoint of other Korean denominations and churches that might more fully recognize women's leadership abilities. But when I went on to work as a youth pastor in a Korean American church, which was supposed to support women's leadership, I found that women were despised as leaders in Korean churches. So I too experienced the mixed dynamics of a *han* and *jeong*-ridden Korean culture, which caused me much pain as I ministered to God's people in that Korean church.

Chapter 3

The Visible Glass Box
Conscientization and Korean Women's Awareness of Oppression

Understanding the Dynamics of Han-Jeong in Korean Culture

IN CHAPTER 1, I described *han* and *jeong* as two sides of the same coin. Further, I contextualized the extent to which *han* is an oppressive energy for women that is deeply ingrained in Korean culture both socially and historically. In Korean culture, *han* and *jeong* are emotional and psychological energies associated with the sufferings of Korean individuals. Whereas *jeong* is a more positive energy in Korean culture, *han* is a negative energy. I suggest that *jeong* can be better understood as resistance to oppression that is caused by *han,* specifically resistance that lacks elements of retaliatory vengeance.

Still, I have experienced that in Korean culture, *jeong* and *han* coexist in what I call "sticky" ways. For me, *jeong* and *han* are like sticky rice[1] because of their communal and group-

---

1. I use the image of sticky rice on the basis of sticky features of *han* and

oriented characteristics. Because of the negative sticky energy of *han* among Koreans, the vicious cycles of oppression between generations never stop. However, the positive presence of *jeong* can make relationships "sticky" as caring attitudes regardless of people's willingness or unwillingness to stick together. Because of the sticky character of *jeong*, *jeong* can transgress the personal boundaries in interpersonal relationships, and this can again result in conflict. However, in the best scenario, *jeong* can foster our connectedness rather than blur appropriate boundaries. Understood like this, through *jeong* oppressed Korean women can experience the acceptance and healing of the brokenness of their lives in the *han*-ridden Korean culture. In the following section, I examine the dynamics of the *han* of oppression and the *jeong* of liberation for women in Korean culture.

Han: Negative Emotional and Psychological Energy

In the Korean language, there are many Chinese characters that sound like *han*. In my book, I am using this term *han* as explored in a Korean *minjung* theology, a liberation movement of Korea's indigenous population. According to Suh Nam-Dong, *han* is "the suppressed, amassed and condensed experiences of oppression caused by mischief or misfortune so that it forms a kind of 'lump' in one's spirit."[2] Most efforts to explore *han* in *minjung* theology focus on the socio-economic dimension of *han*, which is identified as the subjective experience of those who have been oppressed politically, exploited economically, and marginalized socially by powerful and wealthy oppressors. Since *han* has been a symbol for the cries of oppressed people, it also has become a political metaphor in Korea.

In line with Chung Hyun Kyung's argument expressed in *We Dare to Dream*, I think that *han* is the typically prevailing

---

jeong, to express the Korean cultural constructs. Sticky rice is a staple food for Koreans. In *Heart of the Cross*, Won Hee Joh also expresses the characteristics of *jeong* as "sticky."

2. Suh, "Towards a Theology of Han," 65.

The Visible Glass Box

emotional and psychological energy of the Korean people.³ Chung Hyun Kyung argues "*han* is a sense of unresolved resentment against injustice suffered, a sense of helplessness because of the overwhelming odds against us [Koreans], a feeling of total abandonment, a feeling of acute pain or sorrow in one's guts and bowels making the whole body writhe and wiggle, and an obstinate urge to take 'revenge' and to right the wrong all these constitute."⁴ Chung asserts that *han* is the "Korean people's root experiences" or "collective consciousness" because "the feeling of *han* comes from the sinful interconnections of classism, racism, sexism, colonialism, neo-colonialism, and cultural imperialism which Korean people experience every day."⁵

Accordingly, the *han* of women is the deep root of all Korean consciousness as well as all human unconsciousness, because of the shameful and inhumane treatment of women in Korean patriarchal society. If we understand *han* as the "suppressed, accumulated, and condensed experience of oppression"⁶ throughout Korean history and not as the product of one particular cause or one particular historical event, we can say that Korean women experience *han* as their psychological identity on both an individual and communal level on a daily basis.⁷ Because it has been so deeply ingrained in their consciousness, I think it has been one of the primary factors causing Korean women to hold negative images of God, themselves, and others.

Moreover, in the patriarchal society of Korea, *han* has been an important theological topic for Korean women, as it helps to explain the dynamics of oppressor and oppressed. Especially, it is a notable way in which Korean women's *han* has been inherited through oppression by one's in-laws, an oppression that continues as a vicious cycle from generation to generation. For instance, in Korean society, the *han* of a mother-in-law may manifest itself in

3. Chung, "*Han-pu-ri*," 138.
4. Ibid.
5. Ibid.
6. Choi, *Korean Women*, 4.
7. Ibid., 5.

a conflicted relationship with her daughter-in-law, because she holds a high opinion of her son and sees her daughter-in-law as unworthy of him at some level.[8]

According to Andrew Sung Park this vicious cycle is understood as "the work of the accumulated unconsciousness of *han*"[9] caused by patriarchal traditions and Confucian principles. Even though the situation has improved in modern Korea, Korean women's *han* has been transferred to other socio-cultural phenomena of Korea, such as the higher rate of divorce or the increased abuse of the elderly by their children. Andrew Sung Park, a process theologian, sees *han* as the "wounded heart of God" in relation to "the pain of the victims of sin," an idea that helps change our perspective on human evil.[10] Park argues that the notions of *han* and sin need to be treated together if we are to paint a comprehensive picture of the problems of hierarchical society and develop a fuller understanding of sin.

In Korean society overall, the *han* of Korean women has increased through the negative images of themselves created by the use of sexist languages from their early childhood by both men and women. These negative self-images have become embedded in society to such a degree that alternatives are very difficult to consider.[11] Examples of sexist Korean language seem endless. For example, there is an old saying that describes the words and actions of women: "If a hen cries, one can expect disaster in their home." This means women were not supposed to speak loudly or be heard outside of the house in traditional Korean society.

Han also increases organically when children learn sexism by the very words women used to talk to their children and the actions they perform. John Sweeney points to Poynton's discussions of situations in which mothers underplay their own roles and contributions to sexist thoughts of children.[12] Thus, moth-

8. Park, *The Wounded Heart*, 55.
9. Ibid.
10. Ibid., 10.
11. Sweeney, *I'd Rather Be Dead*, 5.
12. Ibid., 2.

ers pass down to their children the view that females are inferior because they have learned and internalized such views from their own mothers.[13] These oppressed women tend to perform the "dirty work" of perpetuating views of women's inferiority, while the true oppressors sit behind them.[14] This is the ironic structure of the world of *han*, in which the oppressed themselves create new victims by perpetuating sexist ideology.

Furthermore, the emotions and rights of women had been completely ignored by the patriarchal dualistic hierarchy. According to Park, this *han*, "the wound to feelings and self-dignity,"[15] has been widely experienced by Korean women when they are hated or abandoned by husbands or lovers. For example, "Arirang," a popular Korean folk song, uses ancient Korean words to express the *han* of a woman when she was abandoned by her lover:

> Arirang, Arirang, Arariyo, Arirang
> Pass is the long road you go.
> If you leave and forsake me, my own,
> Ere three miles you go,
> lame you'll have grown.

Examples such as this show that we cannot deny how much Korean women have internalized the oppressive *han*-ridden emotion.

Jeong: Potential Positive Emotional and Psychological Energy

In Korean culture, the term *jeong* is very ambiguous and amorphous. Like *han*, *jeong* has multiple meanings derived from the different Chinese characters that sound like *jeong* in the Korean language. I use *jeong* as an opposite and a complement to *han*, which contains feelings of bitterness and aggression. I define *jeong* as "affection," or "a culture-bound Korean concept of love,"[16] that

13. Ibid., 3.
14. Park, *The Wounded Heart*, 56.
15. Ibid.
16. "What is the Concept of Jeong?"

embodies an emotional connection toward someone. In Korean culture, the different concepts of *jeong* can be understood by its manifestations in different types of relationships, such as the *mo-jeong* of mothers, *bu-jeong* of fathers, *woo-jeong* of friends, and *jeong-deun* (*jeong*-layered) of houses, books, mountains, streams, and so on. As Rita Nakashima Brock argues, clearly *jeong* is a relational word that includes "the heart of our being, our life source, our original grace."[17]

According to Won Hee Joh, *jeong* cannot be identified exactly with any of the three Greek ideas of love—*eros*, *philia*, and *agape*—but includes elements of each. As Joh articulates, "unlike *eros*, *jeong* has a more intense and vital mode of bonding" but does not include the erotic or sexual attraction.[18] Like *philia*, *jeong* evokes a strong sense of friendship, but it does not necessarily include mutuality of [in] relationships. And like *agape*, *jeong* often engages in dramatic sacrifices for others, but it is not a "self-emptying self-sacrifice" or "self-abnegation."[19] Joh writes that *jeong* acknowledges our indebtedness to others because we are thoroughly relational beings.[20]

Joh also recognizes "the full embodiment of *jeong*" in the ministry of Jesus and particularly in his sacrificial death on the cross.[21] She argues that Jesus manifested *jeong* in his relationships not only with those who were powerless and marginalized, but also in his relationships with those who were seemingly powerful, feared, and loathed by the marginalized. Through his life, ministry, suffering and death on the cross, and resurrection, Jesus manifested the essence of *jeong* seen also in the interpersonal relationships of oppressed Korean women. In this sense, *jeong* can also manifest itself in confrontational relationships in the form of compassion. However, *jeong* does not always describe a mutual way of friendly relationship among the oppressors and the oppressed.

17. Joh, "Violence and Asian," 146.
18. Ibid., 147.
19. Ibid.
20. Ibid., 146.
21. Ibid., 76.

Two psychotherapists, Christopher Chung and Samson Cho, amplify the meaning of *jeong* through its characteristic of "location" *between* peoples.[22] According to Chung and Cho, it can be difficult to understand *jeong* as an emotion seated outside of the individual's heart. They argue that because *jeong* is located *between* individuals and has a "centrifugal tendency," it helps to explain the phenomenon of a collective emotion in interpersonal relationships.[23] For instance, Koreans often describe their special bonding with other people as *jeong deunda*, which is best translated as "*jeong* has permeated," rather than, "I am possessed by *jeong*."[24] Chung and Cho explain that "*jeong* affects the individual's ego boundary; an individual's 'cell membrane' becomes more permeable, so to speak, thinning the ego boundary."[25]

In Korean culture, people commonly experience *jeong* as warm and rich interpersonal relationships that are nurturing and caring, and they are encouraged to overcome difficulties through collective efforts towards common goals. These experiences of *jeong* include the hardships of interpersonal relationships and overcoming their difficulties and challenges. Hence, among Koreans two kinds of *jeong* are often expressed in interpersonal relationships. They are *goeun-jeong* and *mieun-jeong*, terms that are often used together.[26] *Goeun-jeong* is "love-love affection," or simply love. *Mieun-jeong* is "love-hate affection," and is the term used to illustrate a relationship with people you love but who also often annoy you. Because of your sticky feeling of *goeun-jeong*, you cannot resist *mieun-jeong* in your complicated relationships. For instance, because of this sticky characteristic of *goeun-jeong* and *mieun-jeong*, especially when *jeong* is present among the people who suffer from oppression and injustice, they can often preserve it as an element of forgiveness toward their oppressors.

22. Chung and Cho, "Significance of *Jeong*."
23. Ibid.
24. Ibid.
25. Ibid.
26. This is from my cultural understanding.

Chung and Cho assert that "the manifestation of *jeong* in a social structure and value is primarily through loyalty and commitment without validation, logic, or reason."[27] Without considering logical interpretations of content, Korean culture carries the assumption of loyalty and commitment to the ideology of the group. As a result, individuals easily become members of a cohesive group at home or at work, either bonding through *jeong* or held in bondage by *jeong*.

Furthermore, *jeong* and *han* can be understood together through their historical background. Through the many national crises that Korea has endured, its people have attained a spirit of caring or holding-on, which can be described as a special bonding or companionship between the people and experiences they shared in such difficult times. It is because Koreans throughout history have experienced the economic, political, and social *han*-ridden challenges of their lives that Koreans have special affection toward people and physical things or stuff that are symbols of strong relationships of commitment through thick and thin.

However, this affection, *jeong*, tends to negatively shape sticky interpersonal relationships, which foster ambiguous attitudes in interpersonal relationships. At this point, it is hard for me not to mention some negative sides of *jeong* in a *han*-based culture. Most of all, *jeong* can have the negative effect of intruding upon other people's emotional, spiritual, or personal boundaries. This sticky relationship tends to demand the surrender of emotional boundaries and privacy. For instance, in Korean communities, when I do not want or need something that is offered to me, it is because of *jeong* that it is not easy for me to say "no." In other words, to follow *jeong*, some people have to do things they do not want to do.

Furthermore, since Korean people tend to shoulder other people's pains and difficulties out of compassion as a psychological and emotional mechanism of *jeong*, their unresolved negative emotions—such as anger, fear, or self-loathing—can be delivered to the oppressed people as manipulative forms of hospitality, caring, bonding, and attachment. In this manner, some people can

27. Chung and Cho, "Significance of *Jeong*."

use *jeong* to manipulate others as a way to release or to justify their own negative emotional feelings such as guilt and shame.

For Korean women such as me, it is important to be aware that one of the negative effects of *jeong* is a negative and unhealthy image of self. *Jeong* manifests itself in Korean women's lives in the form of self-sacrifice that stems from an extreme lack of self-esteem created by oppressive and abusive conditions. Because traditional Korean women were accustomed to enduring abusive circumstances, owing to *jeong*, their identity was deeply intertwined with self-sacrifice for others. For example, traditionally in Korean culture, a battered wife could not be critical of an oppressive husband. Thus, she sacrificed for her family by carrying the terrors of *goeun-* and *mieun-jeong* on her shoulders because of cultural norms defined for women in Korean culture.

However, in my own life and research, I recognize that *jeong* has great potential to be a "more powerful, lasting, and transformative energy than love," thanks to its characteristics of "compassion, affection, solidarity, vulnerability, and forgiveness."[28] Regardless of the complicated and negative aspects of *jeong* in Korean culture, I would argue that *jeong* can function as a key spiritual practice for Korean women in the form of praxis of hospitality. One important way to maximize the positive energy of *jeong* in Korean women's lives is to reclaim a healthy *self-image*. Like a mirror image, *jeong*, in the form of transformative energy, has the potential to produce not only positive energy but also a spirit of hospitality towards others through respecting the emotional boundaries of self, others, and society. A Korean woman therefore does well to be aware of both negative and positive potentials of *jeong* as part of her healing journey to liberation.

---

28. Joh, "Violence and Asian," 146.

Breaking the Glass Box

Understanding Conscientization in a Korean Context

In the liberation process, we now acknowledge that there needs to be a stage of self-awareness of oppressive characteristics of *jeong* in a Korean *han*-ridden culture. Such awareness makes the glass box transparent so that a Korean woman can recognize the oppressive conditions of her culture. In line with Paulo Freire's idea in *Pedagogy of the Oppressed*, I argue that Korean women need to move through the process of conscientization. In line with Peter Mayo's idea, I maintain that in Korean women's lives conscientization is the "coming into consciousness referred to [as] the process of taking distance from objects, all part of the process of engaging in critical literacy."[29]

Similarly, according to Freire, the process of conscientization is "the taking awareness of reality exists precisely."[30] In his work, Freire further accentuates that conscientization is "a probing of the ambience of reality," because it involves going "beyond the spontaneous phase of apprehension of reality to a critical phase, where reality becomes a knowable object, where man takes an epistemological stance and tries to know."[31] In this process, Freire argues that the conscientization process must go hand in hand with an action-reflection model that he refers to as praxis, for it enables a "person [to] conscientize himself [herself], the more he [she] unveils reality and gets at the phenomenic [phenomenal] essence of the object he stands in front of, to analyze it."[32]

As for others, so for Korean women, this process of conscientization includes historical awareness. By realizing that she, individually, has been oppressed and how Korean culture has historically oppressed women in general, she will also know she can liberate herself if she transforms the concrete situation in which she finds herself oppressed. Freire points out that this awareness does not always lead to a woman actually freeing herself, because it is more

---

29. Mayo, *Liberating Praxis*, 50.
30. Freire, "Conscientisation," 24.
31. Ibid., 25.
32. Ibid.

The Visible Glass Box

related to the extent to which she is mentally free, which is called an "utopian attitude towards the world, an attitude that turns the one conscientised into a utopian agent." That means her awareness of oppression can end up only wanting utopian desires. However, on the basis of Freire's theory, I agree that conscientization of Korean women clearly has to do with utopia, because the more Korean women are conscientized, the more they denounce dehumanizing structures and announce more human ones, and become permanently committed to the radical process of transforming the world.[33]

Like Freire, I argue that conscientization is really the ongoing effort for change just as breaking the glass box is the ongoing process of the "reshaping of reality" with "a seizing of reality."[34] The image of the glass box reflects the Korean woman's awareness of the reality of oppression. I symbolically picture a Korean woman in the visible glass box as the oppressed woman who is aware of the oppressive *han*-ridden culture. For a Korean woman to be aware of her confined condition in the glass box, conscientization may be "the most critical approach to reality, stripping it down so as to get to know the myths that deceive and perpetuate the dominating structure."[35] However, at this point, a Korean woman will encounter questions, such as, "but how can we ever find the process, the how of conscientisation?" For this, Freire suggests "a conscientising education," as a utopian solution as following comments:

> A conscientisating—and therefore liberating—education is not that transfer of neatly wrapped knowledge; it is the true act of knowing. Through it, both teacher and pupils simultaneously become knowing subjects, brought together by the object they are knowing. There is no longer one who thinks, who knows, standing in front of others who admit they don't know that they have to be taught. Rather, all of them are inquisitive learners, avid to learn.[36]

33. Ibid., 26.
34. Ibid., 27.
35. Ibid.
36. Ibid.

Furthermore, Freire emphasizes the importance of "education for freedom," which strives not to domesticate students by pumping myths into them, but to expose our "act of knowing" to illuminate the action that is the source of our knowing, "with the permanent, constant, dynamic of our attitude toward culture itself."[37] This liberating education is not easy because of fear of freedom, which often takes place in oppressive cultures. Especially for an oppressed Korean woman, liberation will take a lot of courage, for freedom is like breaking a glass box with no door, though this time the fear will be related to the conscious and subconscious reasoning that depreciate self-esteem on the basis of cultural standard.

Understanding Feminism in Korean Women's Lives

Feminist Theology as Methodology

To make the glass box visible, we need some methodologies by which a Korean woman can become aware of her condition of oppression. One of the most useful methodologies for an ordinary, educated Korean Christian woman to become aware of and move beyond her oppressive condition is feminist theology. Michelle Gonzales asserts that feminist theology is characterized by "a tripartite method: a hermeneutics of suspicion (critique and deconstruction of historical Christianity), a hermeneutics of retrieval (recovery of the lost history of women), and reconstruction (revision of Christian categories)."[38] By using Elizabeth Johnson's voice, Michelle Gonzales describes these three interrelated methodologies of feminist theology: "[Feminist theology] critically analyzes inherited oppressions, searches for alternative wisdom and suppressed history, and risks new interpretations of the tradition in conversation with women's lives."[39]

There are several benefits of this tripartite methodology of feminist theology that can help contemporary Korean women

37. Ibid.
38. Gonzalez, *Created in God's Image*, 88.
39. Ibid.

experience conscientization about their conditions of oppression. First of all, through critical research on the tradition of feminist scholars who have followed Rosemary Redford Ruether and Elizabeth Schüssler Fiorenza, a contemporary Korean woman will know "the patriarchal functions of the intellectual and scientific frameworks generated and perpetuated by male-centered scholarship that make women invisible or peripheral in what we know about the world, human life, and cultural or religious history."[40] Ann Carr concedes that feminist theology has brought about "the emergence of feminist consciousness," which led to the awareness that women's voices were absent through the previous centuries as well as in the present.[41] In addition, thanks to the lens of feminist theology, a Korean woman will recognize that women have been envisaged theologically as naturally inferior beings and a source of sin and pollution. As Ann Carr notes, I agree that a Korean woman will notice how pervasive the description and treatment of women was in a male-centered and male-authored tradition.[42]

Second, thanks to feminist theologians' contributions, a Korean woman will have a much better understanding that women were significant agents both in the Bible and in the historical development of Christianity. Through understanding the historical research by feminist theologians, a Korean woman will figure out that there is hope for her lost voice as a woman. Michelle Gonzales argues through the voice of Elizabeth Schüssler Fiorenza that the lost voices of women can be recovered by recognizing the "knowledge of women's intellectual contributions throughout the centuries."[43] It is hard to deny how much "women's thoughts and works have not been transmitted and become classics of our culture and religion," "because patriarchy requires that in any conceptualization of the world men and their power have to be central."[44] Ann Carr articulates that in order to recover women's history,

40. Ibid.
41. Carr, "The New Vision," 9.
42. Ibid.
43. Gonzales, *Created in God's Image*, 88.
44. Ibid.

feminist theologians have searched "for aspects of the Christian past of women that were hidden, unnoticed, or devalued yet available for retrieval, if the right questions were asked and the right sources recovered."[45]

Third, to become aware of their oppression, feminists challenge Korean women to reconstruct and reshape theological doctrines and teachings about revelation, the Bible, God, creation, anthropology, the Holy Spirit, grace, sin, redemption, the church, and the sacrament.[46] A Korean woman can know an alternative image and vision of self, the oppressor, and God through this new theological construction.[47] Since feminist theology begins with the experiences of women, by acknowledging women's contributions in churches in spite of their historical marginalization, the biblical interpretation of the perspective of women's experiences will be helpful for a Korean woman to become aware of the male-oriented church as "an institution that denies the full humanity of women."[48]

If a Korean woman can acknowledge that "the critical principle of feminist theology is the promotion of the full humanity of women,"[49] she will boldly stand in a position to critique oppressive arguments advocated by Korean churches. Rosemary Ruether insists that, "whatever denies women's full humanity is not redemptive: what promotes it is holy."[50] Thus, as Gonzales argues by borrowing Johnson's voice, the criterion of feminist theology is "the emancipation of women toward flourishing,"[51] which can pave the way for a Korean woman not only to step into the stage of awareness of oppression but also for her to move on toward her next step for liberation.

---

45. Carr, "The New Vision," 10.
46. Ibid.
47. Gonzales, *Created in God's Image*, 88.
48. Ibid., 90.
49. Ruether, *Sexism and God-Talk*, 18.
50. Ibid.
51. Gonzales, *Created in God's Image*, 90.

The Visible Glass Box

Third World Feminist Theology as Methodology

However, I have found that the perspectives of the first generation of Korean feminist theologians have been overwhelmingly influenced by white European and European Americans, which brought a lot of cultural gaps "by its limited focus and cultural biases,"[52] even though those same feminists have made a great contribution to revealing the oppression of women. Here, Asian feminists can provide a Korean woman with the deep understanding of the dilemma of Asian women's experiences in the oppressive culture in a way that other women cannot. There exist several important networks for Asian women: The Women's Commission of the Ecumenical Association of Third World Theologians (EATWOT), Pacific, Asian and North American Women in Theology And Ministry (PANAAWTM), and the Asian Women's Resources Center for Culture and Theology. It will be helpful for a Korean woman to acknowledge that these several networks have been promoting the liberation of Asian women from the third world feminist perspective, by seriously examining their history and context.[53]

In considering the oppressive contexts of Asian countries where many of the victims are women, because of how poverty, injustices, inequalities, and violent conflicts affect women, in line with Virgina Fabella, I notice that Asian feminists have approached the image of Jesus as a liberator consistent with a "liberational, hope-filled, love-inspired, and *praxis*-oriented Christology."[54] Korean women need to know that it was Korean feminists who brought about some changes in theological trends in Korea since the 1970s. Ahn Sang Nim notes that the education of Korean women has helped Korean women to realize "that theology and biblical interpretation have always been expressed by men's voices, reflecting only male experience."[55] Now, "by accepting [that] what is understood by or what impresses one

---

52. Ibid., 91.
53. Fabella and Park, *We Dare to Dream*, vii.
54. Fabella, "Christology," 10.
55. Ahn, "Feminist Theology," 127.

may be perceived differently by another,"⁵⁶ a contemporary Korean woman can see how Jesus rejected the patriarchal system and set women free. One of the exemplary passages for the liberation of women is Luke 4:18–19: "The Spirit of the Lord is on me, because he has anointed me to preach good news to the poor. He has sent me to proclaim freedom for the prisoners and recovery of sight for the blind, to release the oppressed, to proclaim the year of the LORD's favor" (NIV).

Korean feminist Ahn Sang Nim notes that women are the poor and oppressed in patriarchal culture. Women in particular are captives of sexism and cannot see out from behind men. To such women, Ahn says, Jesus came to preach good news of liberation.⁵⁷ Another Korean feminist, Chung Hyun Kyung, has helped us to become aware of the oppressive condition of Korean women by dealing with the issue of *han*. Since Chung exposed Korean women's *han* under the cover of religio-cultural gender ideology, colonialism, neo-colonialism, military dictatorship, and poverty, a contemporary Korean woman can understand better how her oppressive condition is the result of *han*-based culture.

JungJa Joy Yu: New Contemporary Approaches to the Transparency of the Invisible Glass Box for Korean Women

In this section, for a new contemporary approach to the transparency of the invisible glass box, my goal is to bring together all of the theoretical and theological resources that I contextualized above as the basis for creating a new cultural paradigm of Korean women's methodologies that speak to their experiences in our times. I hope that those resources can be used as a new paradigm for Korean women's methodologies to empower Korean women to both make their dark glass boxes visible and to break their own visible glass boxes.

In order for this to happen, it is important to highlight cultural gaps that exist between Korean women living in the twenty-first

---

56. Ibid.
57. Ibid., 130.

The Visible Glass Box

century in contrast to those who lived in earlier time periods. Most Koreans in contemporary times have a minimum of a college-level education. In contrast to Korean women's experiences in the past, most women in South Korea today have equal access to education as Korean men. Such education is possible partly because of the modern nuclear family system in Korea and because of Korean parents' openness to their daughters being educated. Thus, in our times, it has become acceptable for Korean women to be as academically successful as their male peers.

Theoretically, Korean women and men are equally respected and honored in this regard. In my observation, however, the opposite is true. I am an academically successful woman with various career experiences, yet I still struggle with oppressive patriarchal Korean social constructs for men and women in my culture. Similar to other Korean women, I have experienced sexual discrimination in the work place. Like other Korean women, I have carried double burdens as a successful, educated woman and of enduring sexual discrimination in my patriarchal Korean society.

Indeed, for many Korean women, the very term "oppression" is unfamiliar to them because in Korean culture it is only used for select time periods and groups of people, specifically to the oppression of Koreans under Japanese rule, that is, women and girls forced into prostitution corps created by Japanese colonization during World War II. It is a shameful and uncomfortable thing when educated contemporary Korean women identify themselves with one of these oppressed groups. To those who have enjoyed the privilege of higher education, moreover, becoming aware of the sexual discrimination may lead them to psychological confusion or crisis by disowning their privileges.

As a contemporary approach to the transpiring process of invisible the glass box, Korean women's awareness of patriarchal oppression in Korean culture is possible through feminist theories advocated by women in the third world. As a first step, I think it would be helpful for contemporary Korean women to be aware of the oppressive conditions that women in my culture have experienced throughout history. Then, as a second step, it is necessary

53

to create a safe space in which contemporary Korean women can more fully understand the conditions of oppression of women, both the highly and the less educated. As a third step, it would be helpful for Korean women to articulate the diverse forms of oppression they have experienced in their own lives within a patriarchal Korean culture. The final step is to examine Korean women's roles in current times in light of patriarchy and how it has affected the scholarship of third world feminist scholars and ministers and how it will affect them in the generations to come.

Before I move on to chapter 4, I will share my personal narrative to help readers understand the subsequent dynamics of breaking the glass box.

A Personal Narrative about the Process of Breaking the Visible Glass Box

I am currently a single woman who never got married. As I reflect on my life as an unmarried Korean woman in my early forties, at first, I realize that so many times I have been unconsciously trying to live up to my cultural and traditional standards of what it means to be a woman in Korea. I feel that it has been a gift and a burden to grow up in a society that has experienced such rapid cultural changes with regards to the roles and identity of Korean women.

In my own life, I have not lived up to traditional standards for Korean women, which expect a woman to be submissive to the three major male figures in her life: her father, her husband, and her son. Rather, I have lived in an environment where women have been educated equally with men, an environment in which higher education was the norm for my female friends because I lived in postmodern Korea where education has become an important aspect of upgrading the social status of common people, including women. Unlike the tradition in which girls were less favored and less important than boys, I grew up enjoying the special favor and attention of my parents as the youngest of five children.

Because of this, I have always felt a burden to be recognized as a good daughter by my parents and family. To earn my parents' respect, I worked very hard and tried to demonstrate to them my ability to excel academically. I am blessed that my parents invested in my education and that I was accepted into one of the top universities in Korea. In my life, my family expected I would have a successful career.

However, regardless of my academic achievement and efforts, I always felt that Korean society and the church have not deemed me a successful woman. From my mid-twenties until quite recently, I have struggled with shame and low self-esteem due to patriarchal Korean constructs that not only undervalue but also undermine my academic success and achievements. Because of my pride as an educated woman, I did not have the courage to blame Korean society for my sense of failure. Instead, I blamed my own weaknesses and mistakes, notions imposed on me by the standards of my own Korean culture.

With continuous self-criticism, I experienced a lot of interpersonal conflicts with my family, friends, and some church leaders. I always thought that it was my defects of character that caused these conflicts. I used to hear my internal voices that constantly told me "you are not good enough," or "you are not qualified because you don't have this or that." This negative voice told me I was unsuccessful in society because of my singleness. Korean society disrespects women who do not marry. I did not always feel confident in myself and my achievements. Sometimes, in my twenties and thirties, I could not accept myself as I was and felt unworthy in any places because of underlying this sense of unworthiness in Korean patriarchal values.

On one hand, in my role as a daughter I have also endured challenges to my attempt to fulfill the cultural expectations of Korean women traditionally defined as being a wife, a mother, and married. On the other hand, as an educated woman I tried to succeed in the society as a single woman. However, it was not easy for me to chase two hares at once. So to speak, it was not easy to be successful in both ways.

I have also struggled with the Korean values and norms for women that undermine my own value and personhood because of my gender. I felt embarrassed when I could see my oppressive conditions through Choi Hee An's book *Korean Women and God*. Choi asserts that daughters are "an outsider group who never really belong to their birth families."[58] Even though I live in a postmodern society, I still realize that I cannot escape the countless cultural, psychological, interpersonal, and social pressures that I have experienced as a result of the *han*-ridden social system in Korean patriarchy and hierarchy.

I often felt sad when I was not respected in Korean culture because of my gender and my status as a single woman. I have found that despite social changes in Korean society, the patriarchal system has not fundamentally changed. I agree with Choi Hee An when she states that, "the position of women has not changed for the better."[59] Until recently, I have continuously struggled with my own perception that whatever I have done has been insufficient and less accepted than it would have been if I were a man.

I even experienced that my educational background has been perceived as a threat to those less privileged. In Korean culture, my status as a single woman has also been a source of oppression against me, as others despise me, trivialize me, and regard me as abnormal. What was particularly painful to me was that this gender discrimination continued in the church as I struggled to be ordained as a pastor. For a long time, I felt as if I were stuck in a dark glass box. I felt it was my fault I could not spread my wings in society.

My parents sometimes said that they should not have educated me as a daughter. Because I acted like an adventurous man rather than a subservient girl, from their perspective they often wished that I was a boy so that they would not have to worry about my future as their daughter. They knew it was not easy for a woman to live alone in Korean society. Thus, even though I was privileged during my childhood as the youngest daughter, as Choi Hee An expresses, I often felt that "my whole being began to be humiliated and shamed"[60] by living in the oppressive culture of Korea. I often felt guilty for my

---

58. Orthner and Whitehead, "Introduction," 1–13.
59. Choi, *Korean Women*, 45.
60. Ibid., 51.

parents' financial supports during my education more than they did for my brothers, and this caused conflicts in my family during my twenties. I also felt judged by God because I thought I was not good enough to deserve the opportunities I received.

I continued to struggle in my spiritual journey with these issues until feminist thoughts and a consciousness-raising process helped me understand that my "internalization of the negative character of being a daughter made me feel vulnerable and less competent in everything."[61] I figured out that the sexist language that permeates all of Korean society and culture exacerbated those feelings. As John Sweeney asserts, I experience how sexist language "contributes to the internalizing of sexist images, attitudes, and behaviors,"[62] which leads people in Korean culture to despise women. Further, in a patriarchal culture, women who act "like men" by being brave, assertive, successful, and so on, tend to be viewed as unwomanly and deviant, while women who act "like women" by being unstable, emotional, helpless, and so on, tend to be discounted and devalued.[63] Either way, women are trapped because Korean culture and social norms only consider men to be fully human.

So when I eventually read books by established Asian feminists, it was enlightening to see they had also dealt with experiences of oppression in Korean culture, and that they had spoken of how much the Korean church used the theological concepts of self-sacrifice to oppress women influenced by patriarchy and postcolonialism. Most of these women discuss the oppression they endured as the result of physical or sexual abuse. Until recently, I did not see myself as a member of the oppressed groups in Korean culture, partly because I have not experienced any physical or sexual abuse, and partly because I have enjoyed the privilege of being a highly educated woman. It was consequently not easy for me to put myself in the position of the victim, the oppressed, or the abused in the patriarchal culture of Korea.

61. Ibid.
62. Sweeney, *I'd Rather Be Dead*, 5.
63. Ibid.

However, through feminist-consciousness raising, I began to realize how I, simply by virtue of being a Korean woman, have endured the oppressive *han* culture that is so deeply and subconsciously ingrained in every area of my life, and that this in itself has made me think of myself as an inferior being to men. The process of conscientization advocated by Paulo Freire has helped me understand the multiple dimensions of the glass box in my life: the dark and invisible glass box, the visible glass box with no door, the stained-glass box with no door, and so on. Those dimensions include male-centric Korean culture that undermines Korean women's humanity through demeaning language and attitudes.

When I began to accept myself as a victimized woman of the oppressive *han* culture and male-oriented patriarchal society of Korea, my dark glass box became a transparent glass box. The process of conscientization gave me a way to become conscious of how Korean women become victims of internalized sexism in their lives by the strong influence of sexist language and thought. I felt great shame and frustration as I began to embrace the fact that I was a victim in a patriarchal culture, a person who was despised and lacked dignity in contrast to men. This left me feeling deeply unsettled. My cultural pride began to shift toward feelings of cultural shame.

After I had become aware of all of this, regardless of the frustration and despair, nothing changed because I realized the transparent glass box did not have any door out of which to exit. I found myself stuck in a transparent glass box that had no door to attain liberation from the oppressive circumstance of being a woman (and particularly an unmarried woman) in Korean *han*-based culture. I felt the more I searched for an exit to get out of my glass box, the more I experienced interpersonal conflicts that marginalized me. I was not a "normal woman,"[64] one who followed the cultural norms. Choi Hee An describes: "by traditional standards a normal woman is a person who is a daughter of her father and marries a decent man, who has a husband and children, who stays at home and takes care of children and the housework, who provides a comfortable home."[65]

64. Choi, *Korean Women*, 93.
65. Ibid.

The Visible Glass Box

Thus, in the process of breaking the glass box, feminist consciousness-raising has not only helped me become aware of my oppressed condition as a woman living under the negative influence of Korean *han*-ridden culture, but it also gave me the courage to create a new and more positive self-image through conscientization as a part of my spiritual formation. I discovered that the benchmark of Christianity with "its insistence on praxis-faith translated as compassionate identification and solidarity with the marginalized"[66] could be a liberating resource for me. As Chung Hyun Kyung describes, I experienced that it was important to be aware that "the theological context needed to include the totality of Korean women's reality, especially the issues of human rights and justice within the secular, technological, ideological, and economic aspects of life" for all Korean people.[67]

66. Bong, "The Suffering Christ," 191.
67. Chung, *Struggle to be the Sun Again*, 13.

Chapter 4

Breaking the Glass Box
Spiritual Formation and Contemplative Practice through Conscientization for Korean Women

So far we have seen that in order to break the glass box a Korean woman must first become aware of her condition as an oppressed victim within a patriarchal *han* culture. Second, she needs to become aware that the oppression is not her fault but rather it is the *han*-based culture that has oppressed her. Third, she needs to understand that interpersonal conflicts are inevitable if she chooses to challenge *han*-based oppressive principles. Fourth, she needs to recognize the negative energy of *han* and become aware of the possible, positive counter-energy of *jeong* as a cultural asset. Fifth, she needs to become aware that liberation and transformation of herself, others, and the world is possible with the positive energy of *jeong* and with a clear understanding of God's will for her in society: the desire being for her to have a healthy image of herself.

In this chapter, in the process of breaking the visible glass box, I will argue that this awareness of oppression in Korean women's lives necessitates contemplative practices that act as spiritual formation and a conscientization process that will help to heal the painful effects of *han*.

Spiritual Formation

Awareness through Conscientization

Korean women need to move from embracing feminist theories based on Korean women's experiences to embracing the models of self-awareness that transfer them to a new cultural paradigm of self through spiritual formation. A Korean woman cannot acknowledge her spirituality without considering the conditions and interrelatedness of self, others, and the world. It is because the images of God, others, and self are manifested in the daily lives and in their faith journeys. Anthony De Mello echoes this sentiment for me: "spirituality means waking up."[1] In my case, this was true. Self-awareness through the process of conscientization and feminist principles has enabled me to awaken spiritually.

Self-awareness is key for true transformation and liberation to occur in Korean women's lives. For instance, over the centuries the Korean church has been waking up Koreans to an awareness of their sinful condition, which Christian faith can address. By focusing on the doctrine of salvation, the Korean church has accentuated the individual and communal spirituality of prayers and worship as ways to contribute to the rapid growth of Korean churches. However, I doubt Korean churches have done much to help Korean women have healthy self-images as equal beings. Christians are afraid to accept that the Korean church has been a place of the discrimination against women. It is hard for Korean Christians to speak against the authority of the Bible, which for so long has been interpreted by and intertwined with patriarchal *han* culture.

We need a new understanding of the spirituality of a Korean woman. I believe the Korean church needs to wake up. Korean women and men need to wake up too. As De Mello expresses, cultural awareness should be articulated as an important component of the spirituality of both Korean women and men. For a Korean woman, awareness of oppression and sexism in the Korean culture and church is the important stage of spirituality that awakens her

---

1. De Mello, *Awareness*, 5.

from the blindness of her oppressive condition. As De Mello suggests, Koreans manifest that "the unaware life is a mechanical life," which is not good for humanity, because it is programmed and also conditioned.[2]

However, it may be easier for the oppressed Korean woman to stay in the comfort zone of the oppressive box because the "I" of the oppressed woman can simply be a conglomeration of her past experiences, of her aforementioned conditioning and programming.[3] In this condition, she may feel comfortable because at least she can ignore how much she is oppressed. She does not need to fight for her liberation in this stage of the dark glass box. However, to restore the true being of "I," an oppressed woman must feel the necessity of fighting for liberation. She will find reasons for her liberation in Freire's theory of liberation. Freire states that oppression is "dehumanization" through "a distortion of vocation of becoming more fully human."[4] As a core aspect of her spirituality, a Korean woman accordingly needs to be aware that she has been dehumanized by the oppressive *han* culture and by the church of Korea.

However, there are a number of things that hinder this awakening of a Korean woman. Most of all, it is very painful for Korean women, especially for educated women, to accept their condition of dehumanization, because everything women thought built them up, they discover upon awakening actually crumbles to pieces. Such a woman is afraid to see herself in the glass box as a victim of dehumanization. When she becomes aware that she has been under oppression, her eye-opening experiences will actually make her feel more fearful and frustrated, for she regards the perilous, oppressive culture through the transparency of the glass box in which she remains. She may consequently try to deny the reality of what she is looking at through the glass box.

Some women become so angry about this that they become like their oppressor. According to Freire, in the first stage of this struggle, "the oppressed, instead of striving for liberation, tend

2. Ibid., 67.
3. Ibid., 45.
4. Freire, *Pedagogy*, 44.

themselves to become their oppressor" because "the very structure of their thought has been conditioned by the contradictions of the concrete, existential situation by which they were shaped."[5] The main reason for this reaction is their perception of the oppressed as impaired and internalized "by their submersion in the reality of oppression."[6] Accordingly, the oppressed woman is fearful of freedom not only because the internalized image of the oppressor controls her but also because for her to pursue freedom takes a lot of risks internally and externally.

The most powerful enemy of freedom is the presence of the oppressor's image inside the oppressed woman. Hee Sun Kwon notes that "many victims become fused with their abusers as a way of protecting themselves from violence."[7] Freire asserts that the oppressed would like to identify with the oppressor because "they have no consciousness of themselves as persons or as members of an oppressed class."[8] Peter Mayo refers to Audre Lorde's "oppressor within" to explain the reality of "the violence that underpins the discourse and social relationships that male subcultures display toward the women that share their experiences."[9] By supporting Freire's idea of the image of "new man," Peter Mayo proposes that this is how the perpetrators strive toward their particular ideal of the human being; they create the distorted image of the new person to prevent them from gaining "consciousness of themselves as persons or as members of an oppressed class (Freire, 1970b, 1993 p. 46)."[10]

Paulo Freire expresses this predicament of the oppressed of pursuing freedom as follows:

> However, the oppressed, who have adapted to the structure of domination in which they are immersed, and have become resigned to it, are inhabited from waging the struggle for freedom so long as they feel incapable of

5. Ibid., 45.
6. Ibid., 46.
7. Kown, "Spiritual Resources," 72.
8. Freire, *Pedagogy*, 46.
9. Mayo, *Liberating Praxis*, 42.
10. Ibid.

running the risks it requires. Moreover, their struggle for freedom threatens not only the oppressor, but also their own oppressed comrade who are fearful of still greater repression. When they discover within themselves the yearning to be free, they perceive that this yearning can be transformed into reality only when the same yearning is aroused in their comrades. But while dominated by the fear of freedom they refuse to appeal to others, or to listen to the appeals of others, or even to the appeals of their own conscience. They prefer gregariousness to authentic comradeship; they prefer the security of conformity with their state of unfreedom to the creative communion produced by freedom and even the way pursuit of freedom.[11]

The glass box is the state of unfreedom in the oppressive condition. It tends to resist becoming transparent. Awareness practice helps turn this dark glass box transparent by waking up the consciousness of the oppressed woman to see the reality of *han*-ridden culture.

It is particularly challenging for an educated woman to accept herself as a victim in the oppressive, *han*-ridden culture because it seems that she has been educated equally with men. Instead of accepting the reality of oppression in her life, her internalized language will tell her: "It is your fault when these things happen to you, because you are not equal to them. Your imperfection has led to your failure."[12] Notwithstanding this, her consciousness will keep raising the questions about her discombobulated condition. Then, her consciousness-raising will lead her to acknowledge the reality that has demanded she be as successful as the educated men in the male-oriented society. Now, she is in the transparent glass box without an exit because she now knows why she cannot function as a human, regardless of her all educational attainment. It is frustrating for her to experience this feminist, consciousness-raising

---

11. Freire, *Pedagogy*, 47–48.

12. I express this on the basis of my experience and insight through the compassion practice.

that makes her aware of the double standard of her discombobulated culture.

Awareness in and of itself does not empower the oppressed until the oppressed are willing to wage the struggle for their liberation. The process of the dark glass box becoming a transparent glass box without an exit is only the first stage of awareness of cultural oppression as a form of sexism. However, for this awareness to work as the spirituality of a Korean woman, the oppressed woman "must perceive the reality of oppression not as a closed world from which there is no exit, but as limiting situation"[13] that she can transform. As Freire points out, I understand "this perception is a necessary but not a sufficient condition for liberation: it must become the motivating force for liberating action"[14] for a Korean woman to have a willing and willful desire to break her glass box.

Interpersonal Conflicts and Spiritual Formation

For a Korean woman, it is also important to acknowledge that interpersonal conflicts between herself and the Korean patriarchal context in which she lives can be a great source for her spiritual formation, if she is to achieve full awareness of her liberation journey and break out of her glass box. The spiritual formation of a Christian woman living in Korean society is a complicated process because she needs to combat patriarchy and post-colonial thought in her culture. Thus, spiritual formation is the "spiritual searching process of realizing the interrelatedness of self, others, society, and God."[15] Dealing with interpersonal conflicts is a very important but painful process of figuring out an alternative to liberative Korean woman's spirituality. It is a part of her spiritual journey based on her life experiences of suffering, which have helped her to find God in herself and others.

---

13. Freire, *Pedagogy*, 49.
14. Ibid.
15. I developed this concept during my spiritual journey.

Through her efforts to find God's purpose in her life in the constantly conflicting situations, a Korean Christian woman will be aware of the oppressive culture in Korean society. For this, a Korean woman needs to have a positive understanding of interpersonal conflict as a source of spiritual formation. Since the Christian virtues teach that anger and conflict are antithetical to Christian love, the issue of interpersonal conflict has not found a significant place in constructive Christian theology. However, as Joh asserts:

> The lack of a constructive vision of the role of conflict in human life has blinded Christians to the possibility that love, anger, and righteous indignation may coexist in an otherwise creative and healthy relationship. Further, this negative understanding of the role of conflict in producing needed change has worked against the legitimate protests of oppressed minorities both within the church and in society as a whole.[16]

Bruce Epperly expresses a similar sentiment when he writes that "creative conflict resolution requires a theological vision of reality both as a prerequisite and as a stimulus for the transformation of cataclysmic images of conflict into opportunities for spiritual growth, commitment, and communion with God and neighbor."[17] Additionally, together with the constructive understanding of conflicts, a Korean woman will be aware of the dynamic processes of spiritual formation in dealing with the oppression of *han* and the liberation of *jeong* in Korean society. The disempowerment of women by *han*, which caused women to bring forth interpersonal conflicts, will be empowered by the spirituality of hospitality manifested by *jeong*, which embodies affection, compassion, bonding, caring, kindness, and giving. By acknowledging the importance of herself in society, a Korean woman will notice how to resolve interpersonal conflicts and also how to pursue the liberation of herself and others in her society by the spirituality of hospitality as a powerful tool of *jeong*.

---

16. Joh, *Heart of the Cross*, 100.
17. Epperly, "The God of Conflict," 20.

Feminist Spirituality

In the process of self-actualization and awareness of patriarchal attitudes and ideologies in her Korean culture, it is also important for a Korean Christian woman to critique the oppressive forces of a *han*-based patriarchal Korean culture, which is the cause of personal and interpersonal conflict, ideological oppression, personal woundedness, and marginalization through sexism, classism, and gender discrimination. I assume that Korean women's full liberation is possible by using a feminist perspective. In this spiritual formation process, first of all, no matter how unpleasant it is, it is significant for a Korean woman to awaken from her unawareness of patriarchal standards and norms of women by utilizing the elements of feminist consciousness-raising, because feminist spirituality is defined by women or "those who are deeply aware of the historical and cultural restriction of women to a narrowly defined 'place' within the wider human (male) 'world.'"[18]

Thus, feminist spirituality and contemplative practices through the process of conscientization will help Korean women to fulfill self-actualization and self-transcendence and consequently their emancipation in a Korean patriarchy. This spirituality is holistic and encompasses all our relationships to all of creation—to others, to society, to nature, and to creation.[19] Further, this feminist spirituality embraces a fuller human experience that includes self-affirmation, self-actualization, and self-transcendence for Korean women as well as including an understanding of the interrelationships of sexism, racism, and classism, with a particular stress on female bonding in sisterhood.[20] By living a feminist spirituality, a Korean woman will discover that she is not only a victim but indeed an agent of change and a creator of her own life. She does so by finding various ways to locate the tradition of Korean women's spirituality in *han*-based andocentric traditions of Korea culture.[21]

18. Carr, "Feminist Spirituality," 53.
19. Ibid., 49.
20. Ibid., 56.
21. Maas and O' Donnell, *Spiritual Tradition*, 432.

Feminist spirituality will help the oppressed Korean woman to experience liberation, as Mary John Manazan and Sun Ai Park assert:

> Spirituality is a process. It is not achieved once and for all. It does not become congealed. It does not have even smooth, continuous growth. There can be retrogression or quantum leaps. It has peaks and abysses. It has its agonies and its ecstasies. The emerging spirituality of women promises to be vibrant, liberating, and colorful. Its direction and tendencies seem to open up to greater possibilities of life and freedom, and therefore to more and more opportunities to be truly, intensely, and wholly alive.[22]

Feminist Cosmology

Feminist spirituality, for breaking the glass box, enhances the dignity of women toward liberation from the inhumane treatment of women in the patriarchal society of Korea. But it is also important for a contemporary Korean Christian woman to construct a feminist cosmology by making sense of interpersonal relationships. Nancy Howell suggests the concept of "befriending" as the female connection in its personal and activist dimension, along with Mary Daly's notion in *Pure Lust*, of the interconnection of all being.[23] Howell proposes that "biophilic bonding" is the life-giving connection of women to other women, to self, and "with the sun and the moon, the tides, and all of the elements."[24]

Since the interpersonal conflicts with which I deal in this book are concerned with relationships of women in the oppressive culture of Korea, it is important for a contemporary Korean Christian woman to construct a feminist cosmology of relations to heal her *han* in the oppressive culture of her spiritual formation journey. For this, first, a Korean woman should understand that feminism entails a commitment to relationship. Nancy Howell argues that the

---

22. Mananzan and Park, "Emerging Spirituality," 78.
23. Howell, *A Feminist Cosmology*, 3.
24. Ibid.

most worthy and constructive work is directed toward repairing the damage of *han* that patriarchy has inflicted on woman-woman relationships, although some effort also needs to be directed toward reforming male-female relationships. Howell suggests that "the liberation of women likes restoring mother-daughter and sister-sister relationship."[25] She insists that "a feminist relational paradigm is crucial as a model for liberating relationships and as a nurturing context for the emergence of women's selfhood."[26]

Second, "feminist consciousness-raising," by changing the way women think of themselves, their relationships, and their aspirations, will change the behavior and political action of women.[27] Because changing language tends to change attitudes and practices, as Howell suggests, a feminist commitment to gender inclusive language assumes that thought and the mode of expressing ideas in language affect human behavior. Third, because feminism acknowledges the importance of interrelatedness for each individual self-actualization, particularly with respect to female friendship or sisterhood, what is needed is a philosophical interpretation of the importance of relationships for the becoming of an individual event, including a person-in-the making. Howell says that internal relations are instrumental in this creative process.[28] She emphasizes that the power of creativity, on the basis of freedom of sisterhood, is not diminished by interconnectedness, because it is a power rooted in relationality, mutuality, and co-creativity.[29]

Contemplative Practice for Re-Imaging Self and God

Restructuring the Image of God

Many theologians emphasize the importance of spirituality in understanding culture and society as well as understanding the self.

25. Ibid., 9.
26. Ibid.
27. Ibid., 21.
28. Ibid., 25.
29. Ibid., 26.

The understanding of female spirituality is another important part of understanding culture and society. As Mary John Mananzan and Sun Ai Park point out, "the spirituality of women has its context in the situation of oppression in which they live."[30]

Likewise, in the Korean Christian tradition, the patriarchal structure of indigenous religions and culture has caused the hierarchal image of God to be deeply ingrained in women's spirituality. Among contemporary Korean women, the influence of post-colonialism has led to a spirituality focused on pursuing material prosperity. In this highly materialistic and competitive society, as Choi Hee An articulates, Christian Korean women unconsciously understand God as "unapproachable and inaccessible, a Being without feeling who judges all."[31] In this understanding of God as a God to be feared, Korean women tend to feel that they are rejected or punished by God because of their sinfulness in times of interpersonal conflicts, or when their desires are not accomplished as they wish. They need help in undertaking a new spiritual formation that re-imagines God through their own experiences and allows them finally to break away from oppressive patriarchal understandings of God.

For contemporary Korean women to experience liberation from *han*-ridden culture, there needs to be spiritual practices for healing women by reconstructing a positive image of God. I believe that the liberation of Korean women from *han*-ridden culture is the purpose of particular passages of the Old Testament and the New Testament. First, Isaiah 61:1–3 depicts the heart of God as being about the restoration of the full dignity and humanity of the people who are oppressed and dehumanized. There, God is portrayed as a liberator, healer, comforter, caregiver, deliverer, and redeemer for women, the most oppressed among the oppressed. There is no image of God as oppressor in this passage.

> The Spirit of the Sovereign Lord is on me, because the LORD has anointed me to preach good news to the poor. He has sent me to bind up the brokenhearted to proclaim

---

30. Mananzan and Park, "Emerging Spirituality," 78.
31. Choi, *Korean Women*, 154.

freedom for the captives and release from darkness for the prisoners, to proclaim the year of the LORD's favor and the day of vengeance of our God, to all who mourn, and provide for those who grieve in Zion-to bestow on them a crown of beauty instead of ashes, the oil of gladness instead of mourning, and a garment of praise instead of a spirit of despair. They will be called oaks of righteousness a planting of the LORD for the display of his splendor. (NIV)

The New Testament portrays God as a liberator through the life, ministry, death, and resurrection of Jesus Christ. I believe Jesus has come to the earth not only for the salvation of the souls of people but also for the liberation of the oppressed. The ministry of Jesus represents the liberation of the oppressed including the poor, the weak, and women. Luke 4:18–19 depicts Jesus as a liberator, healer, redeemer, and as the embodiment of Good News for the marginalized in their conditions. There is no concept of God as an oppressor in this passage. "The Spirit of the Lord is on me, because he has anointed me to preach good news to the poor. He has sent me to proclaim freedom for the prisoners and recovery of sight for the blind, to release the oppressed, to proclaim the year of the LORD's favor." (NIV)

Reconstructing a positive image of God to replace the traditional negative attributes can help a Korean woman to break her glass box. The process of reconstructing the image of God will take a deep process of reorganizing the inner world of a Korean woman and of redefining the patriarchal reality of the past and the present.[32] Choi Hee An asserts that "the process of reconstructing the attributes of God is also a process of reorganizing their [Korean women's] inner world, as well as redefining the patriarchal reality of the past and the present."[33] In other words, this process of reconstructing the image of God is also a process of reconstructing images of self and others in society.

---

32. Ibid., 158.
33. Ibid., 158–59.

Since Korean women's spiritualities are shaped partly through conflict situations, this process of reconstructing images of God, self, and others through the lens of feminist critique will help lead them to understand the true meanings of reconciliation. Without facing and accepting the perilous reality of being a helpless victim in an oppressive society, it is impossible for a Korean woman to step forward to take the healing journey of reconstructing the image of God in light of herself. For this, it requires multidimensional approaches that take into consideration various historical, social, political, cultural, and religious contexts as well as the unique experiences of the individual person.[34] If Korean men and women are to wake up and see how Korean churches have indoctrinated them with negative images of God as judge, images that emphasize their sins and further contribute to women's feelings of oppression, and Korean women are accustomed to understanding themselves as sacrificial figures in their families, then they must replace the negative image of God among Korean women with more positive ones, as the biblical record demands.[35] Then, a Korean woman will find a way to become the victor of her life as she faces the conflicts between her inner and outer voices.

Self-Compassion Practice as a Contemplative Practice

In the process of reevaluating God's attributes in light of the reality of a Korean woman's life, and in reconstructing God's image in order to liberate herself from oppression, it is also important for a Korean Christian woman to learn to recognize her own essence, and herself as a precious being. To recognize that her voice is equal to that of men she continuously needs to make efforts to break out of her glass box, a struggle that will make her life all the more difficult until she reaches the point of peace with herself, others, and the world. Thus, in an oppressive and materialistic society, it is difficult for a Korean woman to have healthy relationships with

---

34. Ibid., 2.
35. Ibid., 2–3.

herself, others, society, and God, as she is constantly drawn back into conflicts through her attempts to overcome cultural norms.

In this liberation process, she will encounter negative self-images and critical voices, which contribute to her low-self esteem in the *han*-based culture. The voices say: "You are not good enough because you are a woman"; "You are a sinner because you are a woman"; or "It is your fault." As Choi Hee An articulates, when a Korean woman looks at herself in a mirror, most times she sees herself from the perspectives of other people because she is concerned about how others see her.[36] She feels ashamed because she is never good enough in the oppressive culture. She cannot see herself as a precious being made in God's image because she always feels insufficiently beautiful, worthy, or successful. She also often experiences God as judgmental because she is made so aware of her sins. She becomes depressed and suffers from the negative feelings imposed by the negative cultural norms of Korean society and Korean churches.

Through awareness of *han*-oppressive culture, however, a Korean woman can reveal the oppressor as the one who perpetually condemns her. Herself-image is condemned and criticized no matter what she achieves. To make a new image of herself, a Korean woman needs to learn how to be kind to herself through a practice of self-compassion. Kristin Neff articulates the important meaning and value of self-compassion: "self-compassion provides the same benefits as high self-esteem without its draw back."[37]

The basic definition of self-compassion for an oppressed Korean woman, according to Neff, is to "stop to recognize her own suffering."[38] This she can do by accepting that she is human, that she can think and feel, and by believing that "desire to be happy rather than to suffer, warrants compassion for its own sake."[39] Living in an oppressive culture, an oppressed woman tends to see everything through the lens of her suffering. Neff encourages a

36. Ibid., 2.
37. Neff, *Self-Compassion*, 8.
38. Ibid., 10.
39. Ibid., 12.

Korean woman to let go of condemning herself for her mistakes and failures, so that "self-compassion has the power to transform suffering into joy."[40]

At this point, a Korean woman needs to know that "self-compassion does not mean that I think my problems are more important than yours, it just means I think that my problems are also important and worthy of being attended to."[41] By quoting these words of Tara Bennett-Goleman, Kristin Neff provides a clue for my argument that it is possible for a Korean woman to experience the spiritual and emotional transformation. She is to do this by embracing her pain with caring concern because then "the tight knot of negative self-judgment starts to dissolve, [and] is replaced by a feeling of peaceful, connected acceptance—a sparkling diamond that emerges from the coal,"[42] when she gives herself compassion. To attain self-compassion, as a contemplative practice, De Mello suggests four steps of awareness, which need to put into action repeatedly: "(a) Identify the negative feelings in you; (b) understand that they are in you, not in the world, not in external reality; (c) do not see them as an essential part of 'I'; these things come and go; (d) understand that when you change, everything changes."[43]

These elements of self-compassion practice can create a healthy image of Korean women and God. The first step is self-kindness. A woman must be gentle and understanding with herself rather than harshly critical and judgmental.[44] A Korean woman is typically and habitually self-critical because of the larger cultural messages of oppression surrounding her. She should know that the best way to counteract self-criticism is to understand it, to have compassion for it, and then to replace it with a kinder response. Amazingly, by letting herself be moved by the suffering she has experienced at the hands of her own self-criticism, she can

40. Ibid., 13.
41. Ibid., 12.
42. Ibid., 13.
43. De Mello, *Awareness*, 89.
44. Neff, *Self-Compassion*, 42.

strengthen her desire to heal. Thus, she can decide that, "enough is enough and demand an end to herself-inflicted pain."[45]

Secondly, self-compassion practice requires recognition of our common humanity, a sense of feeling connected with others in the experience of life rather than feeling isolated. Thirdly, self-compassion practice for Korean women requires mindfulness—that she will hold her experience in a balanced awareness, rather than ignoring her pain or exaggerating it. To cultivate the practices for self-compassion, it is helpful for such a woman to "attend [to her] thoughts—interior movements that arise unbidden within a person [her],"[46] by doing "prayers of attentiveness," for her emotions and thoughts, suggested by Andrew Dreitcer.[47] According to Dreitcer, these thoughts include "near-obsessive feelings, images, emotions, ideas, and imaginings."[48] One intentionally needs to allow the self to be attentive in prayer and through contemplative practices.

According to Neff, regardless of circumstances, self-compassion practice will keep a woman going, helping her move to a better place to understand herself better.[49] Self-compassion allows her to break self-critical habits by allowing her to be relaxed and let her life be as it is, by opening her heart to herself, and by changing the image of herself to one that is positive. Neff notes that self-compassion practice actively involves comforting ourselves, responding just as we would to a dear friend in need.

> It [self-compassion practice] means we allow ourselves to be emotionally moved by our own pain stopping to say, "This is really difficult right now. How can I care for and comfort myself in this moment?" With self-kindness, we soothe and calm our troubled minds. We make a peace offering of warmth, gentleness, and sympathy from ourselves to ourselves, so that true healing can occur.[50]

45. Ibid., 34.
46. Dreitcer, "Prayer Practices," 55.
47. Ibid., 36–64.
48. Ibid., 55.
49. Neff, *Self-Compassion*, 15.
50. Ibid., 42.

Breaking the Glass Box

Therefore, by creating the path of self-kindness, a Korean woman can understand herself in the culture by stopping the constant self-judgment and self-condemnation. She can intentionally create a constant caregiving system by practicing self-compassion as a contemplative practice. For this, it is important that she changes her critical self-talk into a kind, friendly, positive talk through repeated spiritual practices.[51] The healing power of self-kindness will powerfully work to soothe the negative emotions and self-criticism by reinforcing the new and positive image of the self.

Internal Family System (IFS) as a Contemplative Practice

In this section, I suggest another contemplative practice, Internal Family System (IFS), which I think may be helpful for healing a Korean woman by re-imagining herself in God. In spite of a variety of capacities of intellectual acuity, musical talent, personality, or inner and outer beauty, an educated Korean woman tends to suffer from self-doubt and self-hatred because of the omnipresence of the oppressive *han* culture. Likewise, it is common for a Korean woman to encounter internal voices that are always criticizing, given the internalized languages imposed by the oppressive culture. The technique or process of IFS, developed by psychologist Richard Schwartz, regards these negative internal voices as seven types of the self-critic, which include the perfectionist, the inner controller, the taskmaster, the underminer, the destroyer, the guilt tripper, and the molder Inner Critics. These internal critics are the major underlying causes of depression and shame and also of the low self-confidence of a contemporary Korean woman, because a Korean woman cannot easily ignore the power of the Inner Critics that causes "unnecessary suffering smothers initiative, wreaks havoc in relationships, and defeats change efforts."[52]

However, together with the practice of self-compassion, self-therapy through IFS can be a great tool for transforming

---

51. Ibid., 54.
52. Earley and Weiss, *Self-Therapy*, v.

self-criticism into self-confidence for an oppressed Korean woman. As Earley and Weiss suggest, "IFS makes it easy to comprehend the complexity of your psyche."[53] It is extremely effective with a wide variety of psychological issues as well as in self-therapy. The first secret of this positive transformation through IFS works at establishing the merit of the critics as an essential first step in being able to intervene in their awkward, painful interruptions of her plans, self-development, and interaction with others.[54] Jay Earley and Bonnie Weiss articulate ways to help a Korean woman put an end her painful feelings and to help her grow into the person she has always dreamed of, without the intervention of a psychotherapist.[55] Through IFS self-therapy, they articulate the importance of the restoration of self-esteem like this: "vibrant self-esteem is your birthright; you needn't settle for anything less."[56]

Because the Inner Critic is one of the most challenging issues a Korean woman faces, IFS teaches her how to relate to herself with compassion and caring instead of anger and criticism.[57] However, one of the important things about the Inner Critics is that "they usually only know one way to act and react," because "they come from [our] childhood, when our psyches were still developing and we were faced with dangerous situations that we were too young to handle well."[58] According to Earley and Weiss, the first dynamics of the process of IFS is as follows:

> IFS recognizes that our psyche is made up of different parts, sometimes called *subpersonalities*. You can think of them as little people inside her. Each has its own perspective, feelings, memories, goals, motivations. We all have parts like the abandoned child, the pleaser, the angry part, the loving caretaker, and of course, the Inner Critic. IFS distinguish between two primary types

53. Ibid., 3.
54. Ibid., v.
55. Ibid., 1.
56. Ibid.
57. Ibid., 3.
58. Ibid., 9.

of parts. Protectors are parts that try to prevent us from being hurt and feeling pain. Exiles are parts that are in pain from childhood.[59]

The second secret of the positive transformation of a Korean woman through IFS is the presence of "the Inner Champion." The Inner Champion is the helpful aspect of self because "it has the capacity to support and encourage us in the face of 'Inner Critics' attacks.'"[60] Instead of arguing or ignoring the problems of the Inner Critics, using IFS as her contemplative practice, a Korean woman can learn how to awaken her Inner Champion to activate her psyches. The contemplative practices with Inner Champion can support herself-esteem and her right to be herself. The practices encourage her to take the steps to create the life she wants, as well as to learn how to heal the pain of her Criticized Child, and how to help her Critic let go of its judgmental role and become an ally in her life.[61]

The third secret of positive transformation for Korean women is through the IFS understanding of "the Inner Mentor." The Inner Mentor is "a gentler and wiser voice inside" the self which is really "a healthy version of Critic."[62] Earley and Weiss explain that the "Inner Mentor performs this necessary function in our [her] psyches in a positive way, whereas the Critic does it in a destructive way."[63] They delineate the seven types of the Inner Mentor for each of the seven types of Inner Critics:[64] These types include the Taskmaster Inner Mentor, Perfectionist Inner Mentor, Inner Controller Inner Mentor, Guilt Tripper Inner Mentor, Molder Inner Mentor, Underminer Inner Mentor, and Strong Inner Champion (vs. Destroyer).

A Korean woman needs both her Inner Mentor and her Inner Champion in order to feel good about herself and function well because they naturally and easily work together. As her Inner

59. Ibid., 3–4.
60. Ibid., 8.
61. Ibid., 10.
62. Ibid., 167.
63. Ibid.
64. Ibid., 173–74.

Breaking the Glass Box

Champion supports her feeling good about herself and moving on in her life, so her Inner Mentor, as "a constructive voice," will allow her to see where she can improve herself by helping her look at what went wrong and what she can do about it.[65] Especially, to a Christian woman who believes in Jesus as a counselor, helper, healer, liberator, love giver, peacemaker, and redeemer, this Inner Mentor and her Inner Champion will know how to have a companionship with Jesus in her inner healing journey.

Following Earley and Weiss, I observe that the Inner Champion and Inner Mentor are extremely important as healing practices for Korean women because the former supports her "capacity for self-esteem" and the latter her "capacity of self-improvement."[66] Thus, once a Korean woman develops and strengthens both caring for the Inner Champion, which wants the best for her, and the Inner Mentor, which wants her to improve, she can risk achieving a healthy self-image, which will not only result in happiness but confidence in pursuing full liberation from oppressive patriarchal ideologies. In this phase, a Korean woman is not stuck in the anguish and difficulties that stem from her Inner Critics in her glass box. Her inner world will change and help her feel confident and capable of breaking the glass box, allowing her life's journey to unfold in an exciting, self-directed way towards personal and social transformation. Thus, Earley and Weiss describe the amazing results of being free from the Inner Critics, which in my metaphor equals breaking the glass box for oppressed Korean women:

> There is an amazing reinforcing quality that happens when you [she] walk[s] away from old patterns of self-hatred. Like taking the first tentative steps on stones across a stream, you [she] find your [her] footing and dance lightly ahead. You [She] no longer have [has] to rely on the tattered woven fabric of self-confidence and self-love loomed from inner support, experiences of successful living, and your [her] growing capacities.[67]

65. Ibid., 169.
66. Ibid., 170.
67. Ibid., 177.

Breaking the Glass Box

After breaking the glass box, the liberated Korean woman, through her personal experiences of liberation and transformation, will be able to restore in herself a positive and authentic self-image that will enable her to feel good about herself and restore in her "a natural sense of being valuable."[68] She will begin to accept herself just as she is, including her limitations or problems. She will be given a taste of approval, appreciation, and attention that will liberate her from her society, which has never given her true freedom in the former oppressive conditions. Now she is going to be "allowed to enjoy the solid, nutritious food of life—namely, work, play, fun, laughter, the company of people, the pleasures of the senses and the mind."[69] Her healing journey for healthy image of self will progress daily through contemplative practices guided by the Holy Spirit and with the help of the Inner Champion and the Inner Mentor, who are there to guide her in a kind, caring, and accepting way. By doing this, she will continue to break her glass box not only to liberate herself, but also to liberate others in society.

Theological and Pedagogical Implications

Theological Implications

Above, I introduced a re-imaging process of God, self, and others through a reevaluation of God as a contemplative practice of self-compassion as advocated by IFS. That process is significant for a contemporary Korean Christian woman to be able to reclaim her true self and God, if she desires to be fully liberated from her oppressive Korean culture. However, it is important to know that God's power has not continued because the judgmental God of her perception has never allowed her to see herself as her true being. Further, because the self has power a Korean woman cannot be freed from oppression until she knows that the source of her power lies within herself.

68. Ibid., 178.
69. De Mello, *Awareness*, 162.

Here, we need to explore the theological implications, in light of liberation theology and the liberation of the self (or ego), in understanding the practices for the re-imaging of God and self for breaking the glass box of Korean women. Liberation theology helps a Korean woman to understand her identity and purpose in relation to God. Furthermore, it helps her to seek changes in the *han*-based oppressive situation, and in her endeavors towards forgiveness and reconciliation, by acknowledging that they have power in themselves, as well as by the orientation of *jeong*, to have compassion toward themselves and others. Most of all, by being aware of the oppressive conditions in the oppressive *han*-based culture, a Korean woman has to learn how to be grounded in the experiences of her sufferings to soften her heart, rather than condemning herself for her mistakes and failures. She also needs to be aware of her negative potential to become another oppressor and not understand herself in Korean culture. In this regard, Chung Hyun Kyung points out that the oppressed person herself can be an oppressor:

> We know that the most dangerous thing for an oppressed people is to become benumbed through internalizing alien criteria and ignoring our own gut feelings. If we do not permit ourselves to fully experience who we are, we will not have the power to fight back and create our own space. We have to touch something truly real among and around us in order to meet God.[70]

Through the language of the church in oppressive society, a Korean woman has to struggle with the message about the unconditional love of God. She does not know how the church has manipulated her ability to accept the language of unconditional love unless both the true meaning of God's love in her life and society's methods of manipulating that truth are explained to her. In this respect, Walter Winks argues that the task of the church "is to unmask their idolatrous pretensions, to identify their dehumanizing values, to strip from them the mantle of respectability, and disenthrall their victims."[71] Instead of doing this positive work,

70. Chung, "*Han-pu-ri*," 53.
71. Winks, *Engaging the Power*, 159.

however, the church has condemned the consciousness of a Korean woman who struggles with her faith in God, not allowing her to doubt God's works.

By not allowing a Korean woman to be skeptical in her faith journey, accordingly, the church has forced her to believe. The church often condemns the woman who is struggling with her faith by saying that her ego should be gotten rid of because it hinders faith. This refers to "dying to ego," the expression that the church often quotes for letting go of self. Usually, a faithful Christian woman feels unworthy because of the church's wrong implications of dying to ego. She feels judged when she cannot let go of her desires and will because her ego was too strong for God to bless her. She makes every effort to force the entity of ego to be killed, if possible. This is the way that Korean women are forced to believe the love of God through Jesus without doubt as well as to sacrifice her life for the growth of the church.

However, Walter Winks argues "we cannot free ourselves from the ego by means of the ego," if we cannot "liberate ourselves from the Powers by means of the Powers."[72] What the ego needs is to be totally reoriented with God at the center, which is impossible for the ego to do.[73] Thus, the ego resists the process of dying. In view of that, "dying to ego" means "crucifixion of the ego," not forcing the entity of ego to be killed. Winks notes such dying allows the ego to be stripped of "its illusion that it is the center of the psyche and the world," by being "confronted by the greater self and the universe of God."[74] According to Winks, the crucified ego, free from the illusions of oppression of the Powers, will discover itself to be alive and organized "around a new center that is coextensive with the universe."[75]

When the ego becomes free from the illusion of the oppressive powers, it liberates the true self of being. It is like dying to the past, the history of oppression. According to De Mello, "if you

72. Ibid.
73. Ibid.
74. Ibid.
75. Ibid.

would die to every minute, you would be the person who is fully alive, because a fully alive person is one who is full of death."[76] This liberation of the ego for the transformation of self can be understood by Winks' interpretation of the message of Galatians 2:19-20: "I[ego] have been crucified with Christ; and it is no longer I[the ego] who live, but it is Christ who lives in me[the true self]. And the life I[the ego] now live in the flesh I live by faith in the Son of God, who loved me and gave himself for me."[77]

Winks explains that "once the ego is disidentified from the self, and no longer confuses itself with the infinitely more vast (which is indistinguishable from the activity of God within a person), the ego is free to play its necessary but subordinate role as the organizing factor of consciousness, designated to lift the contents of the unconscious into the light of day."[78] Accordingly, the reconstructing of the self and God of a Korean woman by the contemplation of self-compassion practice and IFS can be explained by this theological implication of Winks' theory. Instead of destroying her ego and herself, a Korean woman needs to cultivate the compassionate practices to tend the wounded self so that her ego can release the power of freedom to the self to create the healthy relationship with herself and God. In this way, the Christ in the self can be manifested in the life of a Korean woman as a liberator of her soul and life together. This is a healing process of personal transformation.

Pedagogical Implications

Paulo Freire provides the significant grounds of the liberative pedagogy through the contemplative practices of re-imaging of God and the self by practices of self-compassion, IFS, through his radical concept of conscientization of oppressive cultures. First of all, the re-imagining process through self-compassion and IFS liberates the oppressed woman from the internalized images of her

---

76. De Mello, *Awareness*, 150–51.
77. Winks, *Engaging the Power*, 159–60.
78. Ibid., 160.

oppressors. These contemplative practices will help the oppressed women who "feel attached, at a particular moment, to their oppressor as a result of which they cannot view the latter as somebody existing separately from themselves and, therefore, as somebody from whom they can gain critical distance (Freire, 1970b, 1993)."[79]

Second, the re-imagining process through contemplative practices will follow the characteristics of conscientization with a certain educational context because it is the context of Korean women in the oppressive culture. One of the characteristics of conscientization matches the methods of contemplative practices named by Moacir Gadotti: "With the new techniques, a new vision of the world is learned, which contains a critique of present circumstances and a relative attempt to overcome these circumstances. The means for this quest are not imposed, but are left to the creative capacity of the 'free' conscience."[80]

Third, the contemplative practices follow the ways of conscientization for "the creation of humanizing" for Korean women.[81] These methods do not follow the oppressive pedagogy of the "banking" concept of education, because it is not based on the mere "act of depositing."[82] Instead, the goal of re-imagining through the contemplative practices of self-compassion and IFS is a liberative pedagogy that drives towards reconciliation of self, others, society, and God. According to Freire, the oppressed are not marginal because they are not the people living "outside" society; rather, they have always been "inside" the structure, which makes them "beings for others." In keeping with Freire's ideas on conscientization, one of the solutions of oppression can be released through contemplative practices, "not to integrate the oppressed women into the structure of oppression, but to transform that structure so that they can find beings for themselves."[83] Oppressed Korean women

79. Mayo, *Liberating Praxis*, 42.
80. Gadotti, *Pedagogy of Praxis*, 16.
81. Ibid., 17.
82. Freire, *Pedagogy*, 72.
83. Ibid., 74.

will be incorporated into healthy society by being healthy persons for themselves through these contemplative practices.

Fourth, the contemplative practices for a Korean woman is like "problem-posing education" for liberation, because, according to Freire, people can "develop their power to perceive critically the way they exist in the world with which and in which they find themselves; they come to see the world not as a static reality, but as a reality in progress, in transformation."[84] Unlike the oppressive banking form of education, the contemplative methods are more like problem-posing education, which emphasizes "dialogue as indispensible to the act of cognition which unveils reality."[85] As "the teacher-student and the students-teachers reflects simultaneously on themselves and the world without dichotomizing this reflection from action, and thus establish an authentic form of thought and action," the dialectic ways of contemplative practices using the inner-self, ego, Inner Critics, Inner Champion, and Self Mentors will be at work as a problem-posing education that allows the Korean women to demythologize the reality of oppression.[86]

Fifth, with problem-posing theory and practices, the re-imagining contemplative practices affirm Korean women as "beings in the process of becoming—unfinished, uncompleted beings in and with a likewise unfinished reality," by taking the people's history as their starting point.[87] Likewise, they accept neither a "well-behaved" present nor a predetermined future rooted in the dynamic present to become revolutionary.

Sixth, the contemplative methods are very praxis-oriented because they are futuristic and prophetic. They not only help people move forward and look ahead, but they help people look at the past to understand "more clearly what and who they are so that they can more wisely build the future."[88] Thus, the contemplative methods identify with the movement, which engages

84. Ibid., 83.
85. Ibid.
86. Ibid.
87. Ibid., 84.
88. Ibid.

Breaking the Glass Box

people as "beings aware of their incompletion with a deepened consciousness of their situation." This in turn leads people "to apprehend that situation as an historical reality susceptible of transformation."[89] Through a process of inquiry, the contemplative practices direct one towards humanization, which Freire calls "the people's historical vocation."[90]

Consequently, I emphasize that the goal of conscientization is the pursuit of the full humanity for all Korean women. I agree with Freire that the liberation of Korean women "cannot be carried out in isolation or individualism, but only in fellowship and solidarity."[91] Further, he articulates "no one [can] be authentically human while he [she] prevents others from being so."[92] I suggest that the individual practice of contemplative methods needs to be extended to include other Korean women in order to liberate all women from their oppressive conditions. In the next chapter, I discuss how the practices of *jeong* can be an emancipatory force for a new cultural paradigm for Korean women to break their glass boxes.

89. Ibid., 84–85.
90. Ibid., 85.
91. Ibid.
92. Ibid.

Chapter 5

A New Cultural Paradigm for Breaking the Glass Box

Jung Ja Yu's Sticky Rice Effect—A Korean Woman's Jeong-Filled Spirituality

As I HAVE DISCUSSED in former chapters, I believe that *jeong*, as a Korean construct, has great potential to be a positive source of energy and healing for Korean women who are currently oppressed both individually and communally in contemporary Korean culture. In our times, *jeong* manifests itself in multiple forms of hospitality, including acts of affection, caring, forgiveness, compassion, bonding, acceptance, reconciliation, and sympathy. *Jeong*, as praxis of hospitality, can help Korean women overcome oppressive elements of a *han*-based patriarchal Korean culture that has been the main cause of discrimination and interpersonal conflicts for Korean women. This Korean cultural practice can lay the foundation for a new cultural paradigm that enables Korean women to break the glass boxes in which they feel constrained, resulting in both personal and social transformation of oppressive values associated with a *han*-ridden Korean culture.

Characteristics of a Jeong-Filled Praxis of Hospitality

Jeong, as an ideological concept widely accepted in a contemporary Korean culture, can be a starting point for a liberating spiritual formation process of hospitality for Korean women. I suggest this because I recognize the positive elements associated with *jeong*, including affection, caring, bonding, and compassion. These core characteristics of *jeong* can provide an alternative liberating paradigm for Korean women, which I call a spirituality of hospitality. *Jeong*, in Korean culture, can be re-understood to promote the full liberation of Korean women, enabling them to break their glass boxes.

As a Korean woman, I want to highlight characteristics of a Korean woman's *jeong*-filled spirituality of hospitality based on *jeong* principles that are already present in Korean culture. First, the aim in this spiritual formation process of *jeong*-filled hospitality is to "enlarge our hearts by offering our time and personal resources."[1] In my research, I have found that *jeong*-filled hospitality "creates a place where we are connected to one another."[2] Condé-Frazier continues, "it is a space that is safe, personal, and comfortable. It is a place of respect, acceptance, and friendship."[3] Condé-Frazier best echoes my understanding of a spirituality of hospitality as expressed in an "openness of our hearts and a willingness to make our lives visible and available to one another."[4] For me, the most important aspect of *jeong*-filled hospitality is to create a safe space where Korean women are able to connect with one another through "attentive listening and a mutual sharing of [our] lives and life stories.[5]

Second, such *jeong*-filled hospitality can be an important Christian ministry for Korean women. Similar to Henri Nouwen's

1. Conde-Frazier, "From Hospitality," 173.
2. Ibid., 171.
3. Ibid.
4. Ibid., 173.
5. Ibid., 171.

A New Cultural Paradigm for Breaking the Glass Box

idea of the minister as wounded healer, I agree that the first task of a minister "is to offer [a] space in which the wounded memories of the past can be reached and brought back into the light without fear."[6] For Nouwen, this entails a dynamic understanding of the lives and behaviors of those who are in need. Anton Boisen's phrase further reflects on my understanding of a *jeong*-filled paradigm as a theology that can be understood through living human documents.[7] For me, it reflects the spirituality of a *jeong*-filled hospitality that includes full acceptance of the shared interconnectedness of all people's lives in terms of the healing of all people.[8] I maintain that it is possible for Korean women to be liberated from their glass boxes through a praxis of conscientization and subsequent self-awareness of patriarchal values in Korean society supplemented by a new understanding of these oppressive realities in light of the new paradigm of *jeong*-oriented hospitality.

Third, a *jeong*-filled spiritual practice of hospitality can be used to restore respect and human dignity for all Korean women. Condé-Frazier accentuates this shared sentiment asserting that, "the theological basis for this respect is that the image of God is found in every person."[9] In light of this, a Korean *jeong*-filled paradigm of hospitality is reflected in Korean culture in the metaphor and staple food of sticky rice. Condé-Frazier's theological reflection on hospitality embodies my understanding of sticky rice within my Korean culture. Condé-Frazier asserts that, "we were made for others, and we depend on others."[10] Thus, "we can sympathize with the needs and sufferings of others because we have a common nature."[11]

Fourth, in line with what Henri Nouwen suggests, *jeong*-filled hospitality requires that Korean women are able to situate their oppression in Korean culture and how it currently affects their

6. Nouwen, *The Living Reminder*, 23.
7. Ibid.
8. Ibid., 24.
9. Conde-Frazier, "From Hospitality," 172.
10. Ibid.
11. Ibid.

89

advocacy on behalf of oppressed peoples. This process further requires that Korean women be open to sharing their lives with others through conscientization in which she is able to identify oppressive elements in her life for other Korean women.[12] Diana Butler Bass reminds us that, "hospitality changes both the host and the guest."[13] It is my belief that authenticity, as a forgiver and a wounded healer, can magnify a sense of belonging and acceptance for Korean women to be receptive hostesses of *jeong*-filled hospitality. In a Korean context, this spiritual worldview can be a "liberating *praxis*," and "a tool for the healing of [our] society."[14] In a contemporary *han*-based Korean culture, the praxis of *jeong*-filled hospitality can be a resource for Korean women to reclaim their wholeness by breaking out of their glass boxes.

Sticky Rice as Metaphor of Jeong-Filled Solidarity

Thus far, I have identified problems Christian Korean women have endured and continued to endure in contemporary Korean culture as a result of oppressive patriarchal ideologies. To me, this alternative paradigm and spiritual formation can be useful to support Koreans in their search for full liberation as autonomous beings through the *praxis* of conscientization. The journey of breaking the glass box is not easy but I do believe it is worthwhile because it enables Christian Korean women to critique the problems associated with *han* as an oppressive force within our culture. Though it may be difficult to address, I offer a solution to this problem through the use of the Korean cultural ideology of *jeong* as a liberating force. More specifically, I propose *jeong* as an alternative paradigm of hospitality for Christian Korean women to break their glass boxes in their journeys toward liberation from oppression. It is also very important that this metaphor not have elements of retaliatory vengeance.

---

12. Nouwen, *The Wounded Healer*, 99–100.
13. Bass, *Christianity*, 85.
14. Ackermann, "Engaging Freedom," 34.

A New Cultural Paradigm for Breaking the Glass Box

I see both *jeong* and *han* as coexisting forces that are similar to sticky rice, which is a staple food in my culture. The sticky rice effect of *jeong* and *han* comes from the interaction between the two in both private and communal relationships that are complex and dynamic,[15] and thus "sticky." Won Hee Joh also describes *jeong* as being "sticky."[16] Thus, I choose to illustrate *jeong* as sticky rice, because rice is a staple food in my culture and bonds people together. Further, sticky rice, as applied to the image of *jeong*-filled hospitality, means I am not whole if you are not whole, making us co-dependent and interdependent. Accordingly, sticky rice also embodies *jeong* as a relational connection and positive energy that unifies people psychologically, emotionally, and relationally.

By using the sticky rice effect of *jeong*-filled hospitality, I now offer suggestions for creating a new cultural paradigm for Christian Korean women to break their glass boxes. Once the glass box of *han*-ridden oppression is broken, the pieces will be transformed into grains of rice. In this transformation process the catalysts are the contemplative practices of self-compassion and IFS as spiritual formation, which leads to re-imaging God, self, and others. For this to happen, it is important that they articulate their experiences of sticky rice using the metaphor of cooking it in a most delicious manner, and in the process maximizing the positive energy of *jeong* for contemporary Korean women.

First of all, *jeong*, as a flipside of *han*, manifests itself as the negative side, which includes manipulation, control, sacrifice, and so on. In order to cook delicious sticky rice, the positive characteristics of *jeong* should be developed in each individual's case. It is because of the sticky characteristics associated with *jeong* that we humans should not blend in relationship without boundaries, but rather exhibit a sense of our connectedness regardless of our willingness or unwillingness to stick together. For this, *jeong*-oriented relationships should have healthy emotional and personal boundaries between individuals.

---

15. Joh, *Heart of the Cross*, 46.
16. Joh, "Violence and Asian," 146.

Second, to maximize the positive energy of *jeong*—or of cooking sticky rice—it is necessary for Korean women to reconstruct images of self and God. In response to a *han*-ridden Korean culture, contemporary women are inundated with negative images of self and God that have deeply influenced their self-perception and ideologies. Without healthy self-esteem, *jeong* manifests itself in interpersonal relationships as a form of self-sacrifice and manipulation, or as justification of some violence. However, by re-imaging practices of the self and God among Korean women, *jeong* can bond people by creating healthy relationship patterns and respecting healthy spiritual and emotional boundaries among people. By doing this, Korean women can cook and enjoy delicious sticky rice.

Third, for a new paradigm of breaking the glass box and sticky rice, it is significant to note that *jeong* can create a nonviolent or peace-building liberation for Korean women. Joh reflects this by asserting that the presence of *jeong* in Korean culture does not mean that there is no violence or oppression among Koreans.[17] Rather, nonviolent resistance aimed at liberation will have to use "creative and strategic practices" to do what oppressors do not expect. Joh refers to this process as "the surprising force of imaginative nonviolence," a characteristic reflective of *jeong*.[18] Moreover, Joh understands the way Jesus loved as a new way of relating to people that blossoms and embodies *jeong*.

Fourth, I argue that a new paradigm and spiritual formation for breaking the glass box and sticky rice can help contemporary Korean women understand anew the multiple layers of oppression, past and present, individual and collective, that they have experienced, and that this can move them forward to recognize their own humanity apart from traditional male constructs historically defined for them. Also, they may be able to see how they have been formed by various historical, social, political, cultural, and religious contexts, as well as by their own unique individual experiences. Such self-recognition requires the use of multidimensional

---

17. Joh, *Heart of the Cross*, 146.
18. Ibid., 75.

A New Cultural Paradigm for Breaking the Glass Box

approaches that help Korean women re-evaluate their understandings of the selves, to assess their powers, and to reconstruct their realities. In light of the personal and communal experiences of Korean women, they may more fully understand how different understandings of God's nature can damage, embrace, or recreate their images of the selves as Korean women.

It is my hope that a new paradigm of *jeong*-filled hospitality and sticky rice will help a Korean woman find the right path to continue her journeys of breaking her glass box, moving her toward true reconciliation between self, others, and Korean society itself.

Toward Reconciliation of a Holistic Korean Women's Spirituality

For contemporary Korean Christian women to break their glass boxes, *jeong*, the opposite aspect of *han*, can be a source of forgiveness, reconciliation, and transformation. *Jeong*, as an energy force, is also associated with compassion for both the oppressor and oppressed. Like Neff's idea on self-compassion practice, *jeong* as compassion involves the recognition and clear seeing of suffering.[19] In this way, *jeong* as compassion involves feelings of kindness to people who are suffering, and evokes in a person a desire to help the other. This positive aspect of *jeon*g can liberate Korean women from oppressive ideologies, social standards, and churches in Korean culture through a continuous spiritual process of healing. Next, I examine the dynamics of forgiveness and reconciliation contained within a *jeong*-oriented hospitality.

First, by using the dynamics of *han* and *jeong, jeong* can provide channels for forgiveness and reconciliation between Korean women and their oppressors. Joh affirms this, stating "*jeong* has no boundary, sometimes, between oppressors and the oppressed."[20] It tends to be expressed without limit, beyond culture, gender,

19. Neff, *Self-Compassion*, 10.
20. Joh, *Heart of the Cross*, 74.

race, or social class. In line with Joh, I understand an ethic of *jeong* not as a form of capitulation to oppressors, but as a revolutionary change that includes "love of the enemy while pushing towards emancipatory action."[21] In a similar manner, the *jeong* of Jesus Christ also includes forgiveness of oppressors and reconciliation with God. Joh suggests that the cross of Jesus Christ, in light of *jeong*, "works effectively to encompass incommensurable aspects of life: mainly the coexistence of life and death, hate and love."[22] She continues that "the way of the cross must be sustained by living with, in, and through the power of *jeong*," since the cross of Jesus, "with its powerful love ethic, is the symbol of the inclusive relationalism [relationship] embodied by *jeong*."[23]

Second, as an important spiritual practice, I believe that the hospitality of *jeong* can manifest itself in Christian peace-building that includes forgiveness and affection toward an individual's oppressors. According to Frank Rogers, "loving our enemies is an agonizingly challenging practice of Christian peace building.[24] Everett L. Worthington Jr. likewise expresses that "forgiveness requires both letting go and pulling toward."[25] For this, with the contemplative practices of self-compassion and IFS, I maintain that Korean women need to practice hospitality toward themselves. Further, for forgiveness and reconciliation toward the oppressors, it would be helpful for these women to create space and time for attentive listening to themselves and re-imaging God in relation to self. Thus, once a Korean woman creates space and time of hospitality toward herself, I believe she will know how to be authentically hospitable toward other people. Even though it may take a lot of time for the wounded to forgive and reach out toward the perpetrator, by releasing "resentment, hatred and bitterness of

---

21. Ibid.
22. Ibid.
23. Ibid.
24. Rogers, "Loving Our Enemies," 104.
25. Worthington, *Forgiving and Reconciling*, 20.

unforgiveness"[26] to be attended in her space, she can reach to the core spiritual practice of a *jeong*-filled hospitality.

Third, according to Won Hee Joh, *jeong* also creates a "third space"[27] that encourages forgiveness of enemies even in the midst of relationships that are oppressive to a person. This third space can be a rice cooker that cooks sticky rice deliciously. This includes the Christian community by *jeong*-filled hospitality groups, empowered with Christological perspectives. From a christological perspective, here *jeong* is understood as compassion that works to resist oppression and suffering, without the use of retaliatory vengeance. Joh explains *jeong* in light of "a Christology of the executed God calls for a deep understanding and practice of love."[28] In this third space of Christian community of sticky rice, a Korean woman will experience the crucified and resurrected Jesus embodied as "an ethic of love" that includes the enemy "by traversing boundaries between victim and executioner."[29]

Fourth, however, forgiveness is not easy for an oppressed Korean woman because it takes a lot of energy that often requires self-denial and multi-dimensional understandings of interpersonal conflicts in relationships. In her life, she may never experience forgiveness or reconciliation by another or come to the point of forgiveness. In this case, like *jeong*, Everett suggests "the Pyramid Model to REACH Forgiveness" as a medium to replace "negative emotions associated with anger, fear and unforgiveness with positive [emotions] associated with empathy (and perhaps sympathy, love, compassion, even romantic love)."[30] "The Pyramid model to REACH forgiveness includes: 'Recall the heart (R),' 'Empathize (E),' 'Off the altruistic gift of forgiveness (A),' 'Commit publicly to forgive (C),' and 'Hold on to forgiveness (H).'"[31]

---

26. Ibid.
27. Joh, *Heart of the Cross*, 40.
28. Ibid., 73.
29. Ibid.
30. Worthington, *Forgiving and Reconciling*, 74.
31. Ibid., 73–74.

Fifth, to engage in forgiveness, a Korean woman needs to be aware of her positive potential to be healed by fully engaging in the positive energy of *jeong*, which is induced from the negative energy of *han*, rooted in her oppressive Korean culture. In the process of being grounded in *jeong*, a Korean woman will recognize her suffering as an agent to become "a wounded healer," in the process of developing a healthy self-image in relation to God.[32] Henri Nouwen describes this process of forgiveness as a "wounded condition available to others as a source of healing"[33] and reconciliation. In a similar vein, I would like to reclaim this attitude of forgiveness within a paradigm of hospitality of *jeong*-filled spirituality.

However, sixth, unlike forgiveness, reconciliation between the oppressor and the oppressed may not always happen. Reconciliation is recommended for the oppressed, the wounded or victims, to need a third space that should be "given time and a safe space to retell their story of suffering so that they gradually construct 'a new narrative of truth' that can include the experiences of violence (oppression) but without allowing those experiences to overwhelm them."[34] For reconciliation, Ducan MacLaren emphasizes the importance of "contemplative prayer and the creation of safe spaces and hospitality" by quoting Robert Schreiter.[35] They accentuate reconciliation in interpersonal conflicts, in both physical and social spaces. They continue, saying the spaces "must be within what is familiar to victims and where they are valued and their humanity confirmed and where their experiences of hospitality can prepare the way for the experience of divine hospitality or grace."[36]

In short, this process toward reconciliation is likewise important in the lives of oppressed Korean women. On the basis of these scholars and my own personal experiences of oppression in Korean culture and churches, it is critical to create safe spaces

32. Nouwen, *The Wounded Healer*, 99.
33. Ibid.
34. MacLaren, "Reconciliation," 233.
35. Ibid.
36. Ibid., 234.

A New Cultural Paradigm for Breaking the Glass Box

where Korean women's voices are heard, and their dignity with men affirmed and accepted within the paradigm of *jeong*-filled hospitality that seeks healing and personal and social transformation in Korean women's lives. In the next section, I will discuss the importance of forming a *jeong*-filled solidarity group as a safe space for Korean women.

Formation of Jeong-Filled Solidarity Groups of Women

In a twenty-first-century context, I invite Korean women to embrace a new cultural paradigm that allows them to break their glass boxes. The *jeong*-filled hospitality lays the foundation for solidarity groups of Korean Christian women to reflect on the core metaphor in Korean culture: sticky rice. For me, this metaphor of sticky rice holds the secret to Korean women's personal liberation. As I have argued above, most contemporary Korean women do not realize they are living in oppressive glass boxes and thus do not function well—even if they acknowledge it. It is frightening for them to know their reality if they have to deal with it on their own. Because the process of knowing, accepting, and liberating is painful, contemporary Korean women need space and time to proceed safely, and they need to do this by sharing their experiences with other people.

To my dismay, however, Korean church communities for Christian women generally are "not safe places for them to be open about their experiences" or to restore their dignity because they are afraid to be the subject of gossip.[37] For example, it is reported that victims of oppression and violence, who are told to love and forgive their abusers, become re-victimized and the responsibilities of the wrongdoers are easily ignored.[38] As a result, I follow Kwon in saying that many Korean Christian women experience

---

37. Kwon, "Spiritual Resources," 83.
38. Ibid.

shame and guilt because they are not fully able to love and forgive their oppressors.[39]

In this light, it is a necessity for Korean women to have safe spaces where they can be honest, recover their confidence, and reconnect with God's presence as they experience and are empowered to live with "a strong sense of faith, without losing hope."[40] For me, *jeong*-filled solidarity groups are a powerful alternative or a safe "third space" for Korean women to reclaim their independence from male figures and their interdependence with male counterparts as equal beings in their lives. Thus, because *jeong* arises out of the connectedness of human hearts by transcending *han*, it can emerge as a transformative energy within the third space between the self and the other in a *jeong*-filled solidarity group.[41]

Thus, it is significant for Korean women to create or to take part of the *jeong*-filled solidarity group as a safe space for women before and after breaking the glass box, as a liberating process for Korean women who have struggled against sexist patriarchal oppressive ideologies in their whole lives. The result is "the idea of hope for a better world to the reality of struggle."[42] Denise Ackermann calls engaging in this liberating praxis a "struggle-filled activity" that is also hopeful in that it provides Korean women space to embrace vulnerable areas in their lives.[43] Here again, safe spaces are important so that women can embrace their vulnerabilities while at the same time they can be agents of healing through the liberating praxis of sharing stories. Ackermann articulates the power of storytelling for women in solidarity groups as follows:

> Telling stories breaks the silence which blankets the lives of women and other marginalized and oppressed people and is thus intrinsic to the healing of our diverse communities. Encircling the master narrative, these modest stories are part of the meta-narratives of the outer circles

---

39. Ibid.
40. Ibid., 84.
41. Joh, *Heart of the Cross*, 75.
42. Ackermann, "Engaging Freedom," 45.
43. Ibid.

A New Cultural Paradigm for Breaking the Glass Box

emanating from multiple communities of speech and action. They are vital threads in search for liberation and they contain some of the very stuff that nurtures relationships and opens up possibilities for healing.[44]

In feminist theology, a central force is the praxis of women sharing their personal experiences and her-stories. In a contemporary context, it is necessary for Korean Christian women to engage in a similar praxis of reclaiming their voices and being heard in the context of safe solidarity groups. *Jeong*-filled hospitality is an alternative cultural paradigm and the basis for *jeong*-filled solidarity groups that can be mediums of liberation as well as safe places of healing, which will hopefully result in healthy self images and personal empowerment.

In this process, a *jeong*-filled paradigm of hospitality includes sharing sticky rice in the form of personal life journeys and stories in safe spaces called *jeong*-filled solidarity groups. *Jeong*-filled solidarity groups can have a powerful impact on the personal healing process of Korean women by fostering healing and peace-building in the midst of conflicts of interpersonal relationships. Likewise, *jeong*-filled practice can be a model of a liberating spirituality of hospitality, the aim of which is the transformation of oppressive relationships between women and men. This new paradigm of "breaking the glass box" is comparable to the full liberation of Korean women from ideological oppression imposed on them by a *han*-ridden culture in Korea, past and present. Forgiveness and reconciliation are possible for contemporary Korean women by integrating the metaphor of sticky rice into a reflection on interpersonal conflicts they experience in Korean culture and churches.

---

44. Ibid., 48.

Chapter 6

Conclusion

I HAVE DONE A feminist analysis of the oppression experienced by Korean Christian women in a contemporary twenty-first-century context. It is the fruit of personal experiences and observations of connectedness, victimhood, and interpersonal conflicts in Korean women's lives. For me, this thesis is both personal and political. On the one hand, it represents the struggles I have personally endured to critique and reconcile the oppressive ideology of *han*, more specifically as it relates to the traditionally defined roles of Korean women. On the other hand, it is an analysis of core social constructs of Korean culture, *han* and *jeong*, as the foundation for a liberating spiritual formation process that includes reflection on patriarchy, self-awareness, and spiritual formation in interpersonal conflicts, both in church and society. My personal experiences grounded in my academic disciplines have provided me the tools to create an alternative paradigm to challenge patriarchal attitudes in Korean churches and society. The new cultural paradigm is to create a spiritual formation paradigm that can help liberate me as well as other Korean women who share my cultural background and experience of trying to break our glass boxes.

Feminist theology has opened my eyes to see how I have been a victim of oppressive patriarchal ideologies within my church. This has led me on a personal and collective spiritual

Conclusion

journey to reflect on a liberating spiritual formation practice of conscientization for Korean women. In my struggle to overcome personal experiences of victimization, I have come to the realization that the core oppressive forces in Korean women's lives are embedded in the negative effects and power of a *han*-ridden culture. Korean women are not accepted as equal beings with men. In Korean culture, *han* has hindered Korean women from being fully autonomous and liberated within interpersonal relationships. Consequently, women have been the victims of socio-cultural and religious systems where they are either the oppressed among the oppressed or the oppressors to the oppressed, with and without recognizing that reality.

It is more difficult for highly educated Korean women to reconcile themselves with the oppressive dynamics of *han* culture, which is deeply internalized in their ways of being and in their ideological constructions of self. In contemporary Korean culture, even though the social activities of women are widely accepted, it is not easy for Korean women to find social locations where they are fully accepted as individuals in their own right. The process of conscientization and accepting and overcoming oppressive conditions in Korean culture will be particular frustrating for educated Korean women because they have not grown up following the traditional ways of women based on a patriarchal structure of society.

Because Korea is a historically ingrained, *han*-ridden culture, I have found that most contemporary Korean women have not had the opportunity to fully develop a unique identity for themselves as precious beings. They struggle with low self-esteem because of Korean cultural standards of beauty and success, which has never satisfied their sense of what they have and who they are. As a result, Korean women undertake desperate measures to alter themselves in the form of plastic surgeries, divorces, and so on, to justify or modify their low self-esteems. For me, this reality is frustrating because Korean women, whether educated or not, currently live in a materialistic society heavily influenced by post-colonial thought that has sexually objectified them through the media.

Breaking the Glass Box

In my own process of breaking the glass box, I was able to see how the ferocious influence of *han* has morphed into a neverending patriarchal Korean society. Korean churches are not exempt from imposing oppressive patriarchal ideologies and attitudes on Korean women. Unlike the liberating message of Jesus Christ in the gospel, Korean churches are not egalitarian or democratic, but rather they oppress Korean Christian women because of their patriarchal structure, which not only oppresses women ideologically but also undermines their capacity for leadership positions in Korean churches.

Historically, Christianity in Korea has been contextualized within a syncretic process between Christianity and indigenous religions such as Buddhism, Shamanism, and Confucianism. In Korea, Christianity's rigid patriarchal ideologies have intertwined with Confucian teachings in Korean churches to control and oppress women in a powerful western post-colonial context. Furthermore, *han* in Korean culture has disempowered Korean Christian women. It has left them suffering from low self-esteem without having a sense of being fully accepted by their patriarchal and judgmental God. Hence, I offer the image of a glass box as a metaphor to explain the multiple oppressive conditions and interpersonal conflicts Korean women endure in our times.

In chapter 2, I explored the problems of *han* as oppressive conditions in Korean culture by using the metaphor of the invisible glass box. For me, the invisible glass box reflects the oppressive conditions and locations of women in traditional and contemporary Korean culture, on the basis of my assumption that most Korean women have not fully recognized or accepted their oppressive conditions because of the patriarchal ideological constructs they have internalized. The first invisible glass box represents women's experiences of interpersonal conflicts in Korean society without fully knowing the root of their oppressive conditions in traditional family life and historical-religio-spiritual contexts. The second invisible glass box reflects the sexism and oppression contemporary Korean women face in both Korean society and churches.

Conclusion

In chapter 3, the image of the visible glass box represents the waking up of Korean women in a highly patriarchal Korean culture to the oppressive conditions of their social locations. The visibility of the glass box reflects the dynamic process of conscientization and Korean women's rising awareness of patriarchal oppression in their lives. The visible box embodies characteristics of a *han*-ridden culture that are now transparent to Korean women in the shared construct of *han* as a negative force used to oppress them. Understanding the negative psychological and emotional dynamics of *han* in interpersonal conflicts and the highly patriarchal Korean culture can help oppressed Korean women accept the deep roots of their wounds and suffering.

Here, the transparency process of *han* will lead to the recognition of the potential of *jeong* as a positive communal construct and energy within Korean culture. Again, the ideological and communal constructs of *han* and *jeong* in Korean culture are like two sides of the same coin. The oppression Korean women experience, past and present, manifests *han* in control, manipulation, bitterness, and violence. It can be resolved in the form of hospitality of *jeong* that includes affection, caring, bonding, compassion, and forgiveness. However, since *jeong* coexists with *han* it has similar characteristics of *han*, such as manipulation and control, which can break the emotional and psychological boundaries Korean women experience in oppressive interpersonal relationships. Without having healthy boundaries based on a right understanding of self in relation to God, *jeong* can be manifested as violence like *han*.

Additionally, Korean women can liberate themselves by becoming aware of the dynamics of *han* and *jeong* through the pedagogical process of conscientization. The transparent process of the invisible glass box occurs through conscientization, which empowers Korean women by making them more critical of their social reality of oppression and giving them a dialogical consciousness that further allows them to see the possibility of their full liberation as a human being. Conscientization, as proposed by Paulo Freire, provided me a pedagogical and political framework to analyze elements of oppression and liberation in the lives of contemporary Korean women.

The process of conscientization helps Korean women wake up to the ideological oppression embedded in Korean culture and churches that has inhibited them from being fully autonomous beings. It is also a process of liberation rooted in a person's faith in action, *praxis*. In this context, I examined the relevance of the above factors in light of a Korean woman's desire for liberation. This has led me to explore the dynamics of *han* and *jeong* in my culture as a medium for self awareness of oppression. I am also interested in this process as it provides a space for Korean women that would simultaneously provide them with the motivation for personal and social transformation through the conscientization process.

A full understanding of *han* and *jeong* along with the process of conscientization will speed up the transparency process of the invisible glass box through understanding feminist theology and third world feminist theology. This process includes the awareness of Korean women's oppression through feminist consciousness raising. Feminist theologians, such as Rosemary Redford Ruether, Elizabeth Schüssler Fiorenza, and so on, have contributed much to opening the doors for women in church, which previously were led by patriarchal theologians.

For the full liberation of Korean women, a Korean woman needs to start her theology and her-story by owning her own feelings and experiences.[1] Hee Sung Chung accentuates that "feminist liberation theology takes problems of patriarchy and superiority of women's experiences into serious consideration."[2] Based on the Latin American liberation and black liberation theology, feminist theologians consider God as taking sides with women as the oppressed of the oppressed, and they severely criticize patriarchy and capitalism both in religion and society. However, feminist and third world feminist theologies need to be reconsidered and reevaluated

---

1. Chung, "*Han-pu-ri*," 53.
2. Chung, "An Exploration," 47.

Conclusion

in consideration of the different contexts of contemporary educated women who are in a different dynamics of oppression.

In chapter 4, I showed how an oppressed woman in the glass box can now see her oppressive condition through the awareness of *han* culture, conscientization, and feminism. The spirituality of Korean women includes the constructive understanding of interpersonal conflicts as spiritual formation woken up by these awareness processes of the dehumanization of women in *han*-based culture through conscientization and feminism. Even though it is frustrating for Korean women to accept themselves as victims of oppression, now they will know that they need to get out their glass boxes to liberate themselves. But they will find that there are no doors in their glass boxes. Since there are no doors, it requires the internal energy that can liberate women from their glass boxes. Without fully being aware of their oppressive conditions, it is hard for them to liberate themselves. I proposed a spiritual formation process in which Korean women's awareness of conflicts in interpersonal relationships will undergird a process of conscientization. I also expressed a desire that Korean women reclaim their status in Korean culture as liberated persons in a newly understood liberated society.

However, the liberation of women can only happen when women break their own glass boxes. With desperate desires to be humanized, they feel the need to restructure their image of themselves and God, because "the process of reconstructing images of God also involves reconstructing images of the self."[3] Moreover, the yearning for restoring their true authentic selves as equal beings to God will help them not only to see their oppressive conditions but also to accept their weaknesses with generous hearts. This fuller sense of being as a woman in God will be at work in liberating her from the bondage of *han* as an oppressive ideology that has informed negative images of self and God. Here, the practice of self-compassion as advocated by the Internal Family System (IFS) will help individual women know how to restore their sense of selves by accepting their weaknesses as their healing journeys.

3. Choi, *Korean Women*, 159.

Breaking the Glass Box

For this, in chapter 4, I used the image of breaking the glass box because the restoration of the sense of being is released as positive internal energy to transform the self-image and the image of God. I used this process of breaking the glass box as spiritual formation because the thrust of breaking the glass box is related to the spirituality of being in God. The oppressive glass box can no longer hold the transformed beings of Korean women when they begin to acknowledge the acceptance of their being, in self and in God. Self-compassion and IFS as contemplative practices accompany self-forgiveness, which will lead to forgiveness of others. Consequently, by the conglomerated energy of re-imaging the self and God, the glass box will be broken and melted.

This spiritual formation of re-imaging self and God through contemplative practices of self-compassion and IFS challenges us to understand the theological and pedagogical implications for liberating Korean women in *han*-based oppressive conditions. Since Korean churches have portrayed dying to ego in a threatening way, oppressed women tend to misunderstand the meanings of letting go of the ego as self-criticism or self-abnegation. However, the dying to ego is more about accepting the self in the presence of God. One does this by letting go of the negative influences of the past memories and being connected to the inner-self and ego. Through the healing of past memories, the ego begins to be grounded in the re-imaging of the self and God to enjoy the sense of being in freedom.

Additionally, the spiritual formation of re-imaging the self and God through contemplative practices of self-compassion and IFS can be taught to people as liberating tools. These contemplative practices are like a problem-posing form of education rather than a banking form of education because they are dialogical and creative rather than being simply about memorization. By helping oppressed women become aware of their dehumanized conditions and by motivating them to envisage freedom, the praxis practices will lead women to shape the liberated community to support and build up each other. The librated and healed individuals will be healers of others, too. The pedagogical understanding

Conclusion

of the contemplative practices helps us acknowledge the needs of women's solidarity group.

In chapter 5, I explored a way to create a new cultural paradigm for breaking the glass by engaging a Korean woman's *jeong*-oriented spirituality. I found that *jeong* has characteristics similar to those of the spirituality of hospitality. Since *jeong* has the sticky characteristics of compassion, bonding, connecting, caring, accepting, forgiving, befriending, attaching, and loving as a form of affection, the positive construct of *jeong* can be a great motivator for transformed women to create solidarity groups of hospitality. Culturally, this *jeong*-filled hospitality can create the safe and healthy space for oppressed women to experience healing by sharing their life stories. The women in the process of healing can be great agents as healers to other oppressed women in this *jeong*-filled space by recreating the positive stories of women. This dynamic can be understood as the effect of sticky rice, which represents the sticky and *jeong*-filled hospitality of Korean women. It is easy for Korean women to understand this metaphor because most Korean women know how to cook and eat sticky rice.

In the twenty-first century, I believe a *jeong*-filled hospitality of transformed women, nurtured within solidarity groups for Korean women, can have a powerful impact not only on women but all Koreans by fostering healing and peace-building in the midst of conflicted interpersonal relationships. In a Korean context, in line with feminist theories and theologies, it is the sharing of sticky rice—the sharing of stories and experiences of personal healing and liberation—that can help Korean women develop a healthy sense of self in relationship to patriarchal attitudes that oppress them in a *han*-based culture. Likewise, I believe a *jeong*-filled hospitality, as a core element of Korean women's spirituality, will also empower the transformation of patriarchal oppression in their lives and churches, enabling them to become liberating forces between women and men. This will create a new cultural paradigm for breaking the glass box, that is, the liberation of oppressed Korean women from patriarchal ideologies as embodied in the effect of sticky rice that allows them to reconcile interpersonal conflicts caused by oppressive social constructs.

The image of this sticky rice reminds me of the ministry and spirituality of Jesus who welcomed all individuals and loved to share table fellowship with them. By creating communities of sticky rice, I believe Korean women will enjoy their lives with a healthier *jeong*-filled hospitality in their communities. I therefore invite all oppressed Korean women to the table fellowship of sticky rice cooked with *jeong*-filled hospitality. Furthermore, I challenge all to consider the diversity of the solidarity group to make the sticky rice better still, especially in Korean culture. This diversity can include cultural and ethnic diversity in the *jeong*-filled solidarity group as a way to experience the healing of oppressed women from diverse cultural backgrounds and with diverse glass boxes to break. This diversity may lead Korean women to cook better quality of sticky rice because it is mixed with different kinds of grains. This recipe of diversity will help them move on to the tasks of liberation.

In summary, I have explored Korean women's experiences of interpersonal conflicts in a Korean oppressive *han*-based culture thus far. I used the metaphor of breaking the glass box for the liberation process, which includes personal transformation as a way to prepare for social transformation as praxis. We have observed that the problems of *han* have a key solution through the other side of its face, *jeong*. For this, the important aspects of re-imaging of self and God as spiritual formation will create a healthy *jeong*-filled solidarity group and a healthy society in Korea. In conclusion, I illustrate the picture of the breaking glass box as the spiritual and liberation journeys of Korean women. The broken pieces of the glass box will be transformed to grains of rice by the positive side of *jeong*-filled hospitality. In the solidarity group of a *jeong*-filled hospitality—the rice cooker—people will enjoy the fellowship of healing and reconciling by eating the delicious sticky rice. This sticky rice will empower women in the Korean church and society further toward the multicultural world.

Bibliography

Ackermann, Denise. "Engaging Freedom: A Contextual Feminist Theology of Praxis." *Journal of Theology for Southern Africa* 94 (1996) 34.
Ahn, Sang Nim. "Feminist Theology in the Korean Church." In *We Dare to Dream*, edited by Virginia Fabella and Sun Ai Lee Park, 127–34. Maryknoll, NY: Orbis, 1990.
Bass, Diana Butler. *Christianity for the Rest of Us: How the Neighborhood Church is Transforming the Faith*. New York: HarperOne, 2006.
Bong, Sharon A. "The Suffering Christ and the Asian Body." In *Hope Abundant: This World and Indigenous Women's Theology*, edited by Kwok Pui-lan, 186–93. Maryknoll, NY: Orbis, 2010.
Carr, Ann. "Feminist Spirituality." In *Women's Spirituality: Resources for Christian Development*, edited by Joann Wolski Conn, 49–48. New York: Paulist, 1996.
———. "The New Vision of Feminist Theology." In *Free Theology: The Essentials of Theology in Feminist Perspective*, edited by Catherine Mowry, 5–15. San Francisco: HarperSanFrancisco, 1993.
"Changes of the Family System in Korea." *KoreanHistory225 Thursday*. http://koreanhistorydiscussion.edublogs.org/2010/12/11/changes-of-the-family-system-in-south-korea/.
Choi, Hee An. *Korean Women and God: Experiencing God in a Multi-Religious Colonial Context*. Maryknoll, NY: Orbis, 2005.
Choi, Man Ja. "Feminist Images of God in Korean Traditional Religion." In *Frontiers in Asian Christian Theology: Emerging Trends*, edited by R. S. Sugirtharajah, 80–89. Maryknoll, NY: Orbis, 1994.
———. "The Impact of Industrialization on Korean Women's Life and the Explosive Growth of the Church in Korea." In *Asian Women Doing Theology*, edited by Ducie Abraham et al., 113–17. Hong Kong: Asian Women's Resource Centre For Culture and Theology, 1987.
Chung, Christopher K., and Samson Cho. "Significance of 'Jeong' in Korean Culture and Psychotherapy." Harbor-UCLA Medical Center. http://www.prcp.org/publications/sig.pdf.

Bibliography

Chung, Connie. "Korean Society and Women: Focusing On the Family." *Yisei Magazine* (1997). No pages. Online: http://www.hcs.harvard.edu/~yisei/issues/spring_95/yisei_95_30.html.

Chung, Hee-Sung. "An Exploration of a Feminist Pastoral Method from the Perspective of a Korean Woman." *Journal of Pastoral Theology* 14:1 (2004) 47.

Chung, Hyun Kyung. *"Han-pu-ri" in Frontiers in Asian Christian Theology: Emerging Trends.* Maryknoll, NY: Orbis, 1994.

———. *Struggle to be the Sun Again: Introducing Asian Women's Theology.* Maryknoll, NY: Orbis, 1990.

Clinton, Robert. "Life Long Development." Lecture on Leadership, Fuller Theological Seminary, Pasadena, CA, Oct. 2006.

Code, Lorraine. *Encyclopedia of Feminist Theories.* London: Routledge, 2000.

Condé-Frazier, Elizabeth. "From Hospitality to Shalom." In *A Many Colored Kingdom: Multicultural Dynamics for Spiritual Formation,* edited by Elizabeth Condé-Frazier et al., 167–210. Grand Rapids: Baker Academic, 2004.

Dreitcer, Andrew. "Prayer Practices for the Way of Peace." In *Choosing Peace Through Daily Practices,* edited by Ott Marshall, 36–64. Cleveland: Pilgrim, 2005.

Earley, Jay, and Bonnie Weiss. *Self-Therapy for Your Inner Critic: Transforming Self-Criticism into Self-Confidence.* Larkspur: Pattern System, 2010.

Epperly, Bruce. "The God of Conflict and Reconciliation: Toward a Theology of Conflict Resolution." *Impact* 20 (1988) 20.

Fabella, Virginia. "Christology from an Asian Woman's Perspective." In *We Dare To Dream: Doing Theology as Asian Women,* edited by Virginia Fabella and Sun Ai Lee Park, 3–15. Maryknoll, NY: Orbis, 1990.

Freire Institute. "Conscientization." http://www.freire.org/conscintization/.

Freire, Paulo. "Conscientisation." *Cross Currents* 24:1 (1974) 24.

———. *Pedagogy of the Oppressed.* New York: Continuum, 2008.

Gadotti, Mocacir. *Pedagogy of Praxis: A Dialectical Philosophy of Education.* Translated by John Milton. Albany, NY: State University of New York Press, 1996.

Gonzalez, Michelle A. *Created in God's Image: An Introduction to Feminist Theological Anthropology.* Maryknoll, NY: Orbis, 2007.

Han, Gyoung-Hae. "Tradition and Modernity in the Culture of Aging in Korea." *Korea Journal of Population and Development* 25 (1996) 44.

"Historical and Modern Religions of Korea." *Asia Society.* http://asiasociety.org/countries/religions-philosophies/historical-and-modern-religions-korea.

Howell, Nancy R. *A Feminist Cosmology: Ecology, Solidarity, and Metaphysics.* Amherst, NY: Humanity, 2000.

Ingram, Paul O., editor. *Constructing a Relational Cosmology.* Eugene, OR: Pickwick, 2006.

Joh, Wonhee Ann. *Heart of the Cross: A Postcolonial Christology.* Louisville: Westminster John Knox, 2006.

Bibliography

———. "Violence and Asian American Experience." In *Off the Menu: Asian and Asian North American Women's Religion and Theology*, edited by Rita Nakashima Brock et al., 145–62. Louisville: Westminster John Knox, 2007.

Johnson, Allan G. "Misogyny." In *Blackwell Dictionary of Sociology: A User's Guide to Sociological Language*. Oxford: Blackwell, 2000.

Jung, Ji-Sung. "Women's Unequal Access to Education in South Korea." *Comparative Education Review* 38:4 (1994) 487.

Kang, Nam-Sun. "Confucian Familism and its Social/Religious Embodiment in Christianity: Reconsidering the Family Discourse from a Feminist Perspective." *Asia Journal of Theology* 18:1 (2004) 173.

Kelleher, Theresa. "Confucianism." In *Women in World Religions*, edited by Arvind Sharma. Albany: State University of New York Press, 1987.

Kown, Hee Sun. "Spiritual Resources Used By Korean Victims of Domestic Violence." *Journal of Pastoral Theology* 14:2 (2004) 72.

Kwok, Pui-lan. "Fishing the Asian Pacific: Transnationalism and Feminist Theology." In *Off the Menu: Asian and Asian North American Women's Religion and Theology*, edited by Rita Nakashima Brock et al., 3–22. Louisville: Westminster John Knox, 2007.

Lee, Yu-Jin. *The Meaning of Korean Women's Career-Leaving Experience*. Proquest: UMI Dissertation, 2011.

Maas, Robin, and Gabriel O' Donnell. *Spiritual Traditions for the Contemporary Church*. Nashville: Abingdon, 1990.

MacLaren, Duncan. "Reconciliation: Linking Spirituality with Development." *Studies in World Christianity* 9:2 (2003) 233.

Mananzan, Mary John, and Sun Ai Park. "Emerging Spirituality of Asian Women." In *With Passion and Compassion: Third World Women Doing Theology*. Maryknoll, NY: Orbis, 1988.

"Marriage in South Korea." http://en.wikipedia.org/wiki/Marriage_in_South_Korea.

May, Gerald G. *Will and Spirit: A Contemplative Psychology*. San Francisco: Harper & Row, 1982.

Mayo, Peter. *Liberating Praxis: Paulo Freire's Legacy for Radical Education and Politics*. London: Praeger, 2004.

Mello, Anthony De. *Awareness: The Perils and Opportunities of Reality*. New York: Doubleday, 1992.

Neff, Kristin. *Self-Compassion: Stop Beating Yourself Up and Leave Insecurity Behind*. New York: HarperCollins, 2011.

Nouwen, Henri J. M. *The Living Reminder: Service and Prayer in Memory of Jesus Christ*. New York: Crossroad, 1977.

———. *The Wounded Healer: Ministry in Contemporary Society*. New York: Doubleday, 1990.

Orthner, Sherry B., and Harriet Whitehead. "Introduction: Accounting for Sexual Meanings." In *Sexual Meanings: The Cultural Construction of Gender and Sexuality*, edited by Sherry B. Ortner and Harriet Whitehead. Cambridge: Cambridge University Press, 1981.

Bibliography

Park, Andrew Sung. *The Wounded Heart of God: The Asian Concept of Han and the Christian Doctrine of Sin*. Nashville: Abingdon, 1993.

"Profiting from Sexism." *The Economist*. No pages. Online: http://www.economist.com/node/17311877

Rogers, Frank. "Loving Our Enemies: Contributions of the Narrative Arts to the Practice of Peacebuilding." In *Choosing Peace through Daily Practices*, edited by Ellen Ott Marshall, 86–105. Cleveland: Pilgrim, 2005.

Ruether, Rosemary Radford. *Sexism and God-Talk: Toward a Feminist Theology*. Boston: Beacon, 1983.

Schroeder, Edward H. Review of *Korean Women Search for the Silver Coin* by Young Kim. *The Christian Century* 107:15 (1990).

Sherrd, Andrea. Comment on the guest blog of Fiedel Hart. "An Ugly Reflection: Plastic Surgery in Korea." *Follow Your Hart Blog*. http://www.scenewithahart.com/asia/korea-asia/plasticsurgery/.

"South Korea Tops Plastic Surgery Tables Again, Netizens React." *Korea Bang*. No pages. Online: http://www.koreabang.com/2012/stories/south-korea-tops-plastic-surgery-tables-again-netizens-react.html.

Suh, Nam Dong. "Toward a Theology of Han." In *Minjung Theology: People as the Subjects of History*, edited by The Commission on Theological Concerns of the Christian Conference of Asia. Maryknoll, NY: Orbis, 1981.

Sweeney, John M. *I'd Rather Be Dead Than Be a Girl: Implications of Whitehead, Whorf, and Piaget for Inclusive Language in Religious Education*. New York: University Press of America, 2009.

"What is the Concept of Jeong?" http://answers.yahoo.com/question/index?qid=20071015133022AAAEukc.

Winks, Walter. *Engaging the Power: Discernment and Resistance in a World of Dominion*. Minneapolis: Fortress, 1992.

"Women in South Korea." http://en.wikipedia.org/wiki/Women_in_South_Korea.

"Women's Role in Contemporary Korea." *Asia Society*. http://asiasociety.org/countries/traditions/womens-role-contemporary-korea.

Worthington, Everett L. Jr. *Forgiving and Reconciling: Bridges to Wholeness and Hope*. Downers Grove, IL: InterVarsity, 2001.

Yi, Hyo-Jae. "Christian Mission and the Liberation of Korean Women." *International Review of Mission* 70 (1985) 93.

www.ingramcontent.com/pod-product-compliance
Lightning Source LLC
Chambersburg PA
CBHW050838160426
43192CB00011B/2069